C000180845

Shoe Leather Faith

A devotional daily commentary
on the letter of James

Alan Hoare

Onwards and Upwards Publishers

3 Radfords Turf, Cranbrook, Exeter, EX5 7DX.

www.onwardsandupwards.org

Copyright © Alan Hoare 2017

The right of Alan Hoare to be identified as the author of this work has been asserted by the author in accordance with the Copyright, Designs and Patents Act 1988.

All rights reserved.

No part of this publication may be reproduced or transmitted in any form or by any means, electronic or mechanical, including photocopy, recording or any information storage and retrieval system, without permission in writing from the author or publisher.

Printed in the UK.

ISBN:	978-1-911086-73-4
Typeface:	Sabon LT
Graphic design:	LM Graphic Designer

Every effort has been made to trace copyright holders but if any have inadvertently been overlooked, the author and publishers will be pleased to make the necessary amendments to future reprints and editions of this book.

Unless otherwise indicated, all Scripture quotations are from the ESV® Bible (The Holy Bible, English Standard Version®), copyright © 2001 by Crossway, a publishing ministry of Good News Publishers. Used by permission. All rights reserved.

Scripture quotations marked (Jerusalem Bible) are from The Jerusalem Bible, copyright © 1966 by Darton, Longman & Todd, Ltd. and Doubleday, a division of Bantam Doubleday Dell Publishing Group, Inc. Reprinted by permission.

Scripture quotations marked (Living Bible) are taken from The Living Bible copyright © 1971. Used by permission of Tyndale House Publishers, Inc., Carol Stream, Illinois 60188. All rights reserved.

Scripture quotations marked (Moffatt) are from A New Translation of the Bible, Containing the Old and New Testaments by James Moffatt. New York: Doran, 1926. Revised edition, New York and London: Harper and Brothers, 1935. Reprinted, Grand Rapids: Kregel, 1995.

Scripture quotations marked (MSG) or (The Message) are taken from The Message. Copyright 1993, 1994, 1995, 1996, 2000, 2001, 2002. Used by permission of NavPress Publishing Group.

Scripture quotations marked (NASB) are taken from the New American Standard Bible® (NASB), Copyright © 1960, 1962, 1963, 1968, 1971, 1972, 1973, 1975, 1977, 1995 by The Lockman Foundation. Used by permission. www.Lockman.org

Scripture quotations marked (NIV) are taken from the Holy Bible, NEW INTERNATIONAL VERSION®, NIV® Copyright © 1973, 1978, 1984, 2011 by Biblica, Inc.® Used by permission. All rights reserved worldwide.

Scripture quotations marked (NLT) are taken from the Holy Bible, New Living Translation, copyright © 1996. Used by permission of Tyndale House Publishers, Inc., Wheaton, Illinois 60189. All rights reserved.

Scripture quotations marked (PHI) or (J.B. Phillips) are taken from The New Testament in Modern English by J. B. Phillips, copyright © J. B. Phillips, 1958, 1959, 1960, 1972. All rights reserved.

Scripture quotations marked (Weymouth) are from Weymouth New Testament in Modern Speech, Third Edition.

Scripture quotations marked (Wuest) are from The New Testament: An Expanded Translation by Kenneth S. Wuest

Endorsements

'Shoe Leather Faith' is the latest offering of daily devotional readings from my friend Pastor Alan Hoare. For me, when Alan Hoare is mentioned, his pastoral heart and gift truly authenticates his writing. This is obviously a well-researched book. Here, the life and times, the world views and cultures surrounding James the apostle are clearly interpreted. Including seemingly bizarre observations such as the aside that the prayer life of James was such that his knees resembled those of a camel! James was a man who spent much of his life on his knees! However, it's the profound insight and reflections that come from Alan's lifetime of spiritual soaking and biblical integrity that bring to the reader challenge and hope, awareness and awe! I commend this book as a rich source of a deepening dependency on Christ and insight into his divine purposes.

Rev Canon **Chris Bowater** OSL
Retired Pastor; worship leader, mentor, musician, author and teacher
Co-founder of Worship Academy International

Alan's love for God and his people shines through his latest devotional, 'Shoe Leather Faith'. As you study his writings, you'll hear the voice of Jesus beckoning you into a closer walk with him. Alan's mission is to build strong Christians, steeped in God's Word; he certainly succeeds in this book, and I strongly recommend it to you.

Laurie Mellor
Head of Practice, The Mellor Practice, LighthouseWealth Limited
http://themellorpractice.co.uk

My own spiritual journey benefited enormously from Alan's enthusiastic passion for explaining the Scriptures to me as a friend. I wholeheartedly recommend his daily devotional: bite-sized nuggets of easy-to-understand yet challenging and life-changing theology. Great stuff!

Andy Piercy
Singer / Songwriter; Worship Consultant; Record Producer

Having worked alongside Alan for many years I have benefited from his excellent teaching gift in numerous ways. Whether in short daily devotions or in the preparing of materials on complex theological issues, Alan has faithfully devoted himself to teach God's word. These studies in James again reveal his attention to detail and his ability to 'rightly handle words of truth'. He loves to make the Bible accessible to all. I believe these daily studies will be a blessing to many.

Stuart Bell
Senior Pastor, Alive Church, Lincoln
Leader, Ground Level Network

Alan Hoare is one of the most devoted students of Scripture I've been blessed to know, not just for his learning's sake but for his passionate belief in its power to effect godly change in our lives. As a long-time friend and colleague, few men that I've known have so consistently put aside time to 'mine' Scripture for all its worth. The result is a disciple of Christ who can unpeel Scripture in layers, revealing God's imminent presence through his Spirit-breathed Word.

Johnny Markin
Worship Pastor / Songwriter,
Northview Community Church, Abbotsford, Canada

About the Author

Alan was born in Rustington in West Sussex in 1948, and was followed by two younger brothers, Nigel and Simon. His first experience of church ended a few weeks later by him being banned from the local Sunday school for bad behaviour! After leaving school he did an apprenticeship in precision engineering, gaining City and Guilds certificates at Worthing Technical College. It was the 'hippy' era of the 1960s, so weekends were spent with friends, often performing in their rock band, aptly named the 'St James' Infirmary'. A favourite pastime of his is still to pick up his guitar and play the music of that era.

Life changed dramatically for him in March 1969 when he became a Christian as the result of visiting a small Free Church in the little village of Fittleworth, near Petworth. Soon after that, the Baptist Church in Littlehampton became his home church, and also the place where he met Maureen (affectionately known as Mo), who was to become his wife in 1974. Before that, however, they parted company for two years – he to work on a church planting team with Operation Mobilisation in France for two years, and she to do teacher training in Portsmouth.

On returning to England in 1973, Alan studied theology at the Elim Bible College, which was then in Dorking in Surrey, for two years, graduating with a Diploma in Theology. Marriage took place in the middle of the course – highly unusual in those days! This was followed by two years in London, during which time he was an assistant minister at two Elim Pentecostal churches, helped to pioneer two more churches and had two children: Ruth, who was born prematurely in August 1975, and Joseph, who was born in February 1977.

August 1977 saw a move to Lincoln, where he took up the pastorate of an Elim Pentecostal church for nearly ten years. The family meanwhile grew with the added births of Simon in November 1980 and Sarah in March 1982. The family home was an open house, with many visitors staying overnight or for various periods of time.

In Lincoln, Alan quickly developed a strong connection with Stuart Bell, the leader of the large and growing New Life Church there (now 'Alive Church'), and was one of the founder members of the Ground Level network of churches which Stuart started and still leads. In 1987 he joined the New Life Church himself, serving as a member until 1991, when he joined the staff as part of the leadership team. His role was to head up the pastoral and teaching ministry of the church. Benjamin, his youngest son, was born in November that year, completing their family – a biblical quiver full!

In his work for the New Life church, Alan has also, amongst other things, pastored a number of linked congregations around the area, written and delivered staff devotions, led marriage preparation, baptismal and membership courses. He is currently teaching 'X-Plore' classes in a number of different churches. Topics covered in this course have included, amongst others, 'The Life and Times of Christ', 'The Life and Times of David', 'The Life of the Apostle Paul', 'Spiritual Theology', 'Systematic Theology' and 'Church History'.

Alan had always dreamt of studying for a degree in theology, and was delighted that the church released him one day a week in 2009 so that he could do this. He attended Mattersey Hall near Doncaster, and was accepted on to the Masters course, graduating three years later. For a number of years, he was a contributor for Scripture Union's online WordLive daily devotions.

In 2011, he reduced his time at Lincoln to three days a week, and took on a new role as the senior pastor of a thriving church in Boston, some forty miles east of Lincoln. After three years working for them two days a week, he helped them with the transition to a new senior pastor, and now serves on their leadership team just one day a week as their teaching pastor.

On reaching retirement age in August 2013, Alan retired completely from the staff at Lincoln, and is now able to devote himself more to study, writing and teaching. He has since been teaching in churches both in the Lincolnshire area and abroad. Over the years, he has taught the Scriptures in Mozambique, Vietnam, France, Spain, Poland and Greece. He is currently teaching three different courses in three different churches. Retiring is not in his vocabulary!

Alan feels that his ministry is primarily about building strong and deep spiritual foundations. Strong and mature churches, in his view, are made up of strong and mature believers. He teaches about developing a close and mature walk with Christ, believing that spiritual roots are essential to growing a healthy Christian life. He is passionate about getting people to read the Bible for themselves!

Alan and Mo have now been married for over forty years, and have seen their five children grow up into fine adults. They have, to date, eleven grandchildren!

Alan Hoare can be contacted by email:

alanerichoare@gmail.com

To see all the author's books published by
Onwards and Upwards, visit his author page:

www.onwardsandupwards.org/brand/hoare-alan

Or scan the barcode below with your smartphone:

Preface

For well over 1,500 years, there has been a spiritual practice in many quarters of the church known in Latin as lectio divina or 'sacred reading'. In a nutshell, the practice of lectio divina was the careful and prayerful, slow, deliberate and thoughtful reading and meditating in the Scriptures. The goal of lectio divina was to see the Word of God becoming somehow incarnated into the lives of those who gave attention to this ancient practice.

It seems that there is a rediscovery of lectio divina happening these days. Maybe many are tired of the frenetic pace at which life is lived today, and of a superficial grasp of the Scriptures, and are seeking to slow down, at least on the inside, and to find again the richness of deeply soaking themselves in the world and the words of the Bible.

Lectio divina is not a case of how much we read but how deeply we read. With this practice, we read carefully and slowly, pondering the words at depth and chewing over each phrase, turning our informed thoughts into prayer, and finding ourselves getting caught up in fresh visions of God and his beautiful kingdom.

For decades now, I have read the Scriptures over and over, but I also have learned at times to pause and to listen to the voice of God that can be heard through them. We all know that the Scriptures are "living and active" (Heb.4:12), and that through them God speaks to us and imparts his life into us. In fact, Professor Eugene Peterson encourages us to carefully read the Scriptures, not so much with our eyes, but with our spiritual ears. King David wrote in Psa.40:6:

> *In sacrifice and offering you have not delighted, but you have given me an open ear. Burnt offering and sin offering you have not required.*

The phrase "you have given me an open ear" is more literally 'you have dug out my ear'. The Hebrew word is 'kârâh', and it means 'to dig, to excavate, to dig through'.

Commenting on this verse, Peterson writes:

> *So God gets a pick and a shovel and digs through the cranial granite, opening a passage that will give access to the*

interior depths, into the mind and heart. Or, maybe, we are not to imagine a smooth expanse of skull, but something like wells that have been stopped up with refuse: culture noise, throw away gossip, garbage chatter. Our ears are so clogged up that we cannot hear God speak. God, like Isaac, who dug again the wells that the Philistines had filled, re-digs the ears trashed with audio junk. The result is a restoration of scripture: eyes turn into ears.[1]

In one sense, I have spent nearly a year with James. These daily readings in his letter to the church have come out of wonderful hours of reading and soaking up his words, trying to get into his world in order to exegete the meanings of the words and phrases that he uses, and then seeking to build a hermeneutical bridge in order to open and explain what have become timeless truths to this world we find ourselves living in today.

In the introduction to his letter in the New Inductive Study Bible, I found this little phrase that caught my attention and, in my view, described very accurately its purpose – this letter that James wrote was "an epistle that would show what the gospel is like when it is lived out in shoe leather"[2]. Hence the title – 'Shoe Leather Faith'! The faith that James wrote about was a faith that is not merely a cerebral affair, but one that is to be believed, experienced and worked out in the nitty-gritty of life at ground-level.

These little studies and meditations are specifically designed to come alongside your own ordinary reading of the Scriptures. They are not meant to be an alternative, but an add-on if you like. They will encourage you to slow down, and take your time over one or two verses at a time, hopefully allowing them to sink deeply into your heart and spirit. May you pick up the heart of James as you spend time with him.

---

[1]   Eugene H. Peterson, *Working the Angles*, (Eerdmans, Michigan, 1995), pp.101,102

[2]   *The New ESV Inductive Study Bible*, (Harvest House Publishers, Oregon, 2013), p.2082

DAY ONE

James the Half-Brother

1:1a (NLT)

...from James, a slave of God and of the Lord Jesus Christ.

We are going to spend some time each morning looking at this letter written by James. Much evidence points to this being the earliest piece of New Testament writing, dated somewhere between AD44 and AD49. Out of interest, unlike the letter we see in the Bible, his original letter would not have had any chapter or verse divisions, and would have been written in capitals.

But first of all, I would like us to think of James himself. The Bible tells us that he was the half-brother of Jesus. One early source says that he was the youngest son of Joseph. I want us to imagine for a moment what it must have been like growing up in the home with Jesus as your elder brother. The interesting and sad thing is that none of Jesus' brothers believed in him, as John records for us in his Gospel.[3] Jesus, the firstborn, lived in the family carpenter shop for thirty years, and one by one, he was joined by his various brothers and sisters. Whether it was sibling rivalry, or that his holy living produced resentment or jealousy in them, we shall never know. Were they too close? Was it the fact that a prophet is not without honour in his own home? Mary and Joseph certainly knew who he was. Had they told the kids? Did Jesus tell them himself? The fact remains: they (and James among them) did not believe in him.

From what we can deduce from the biblical record, Jesus appeared specifically to James after the resurrection, and he was subsequently found in the prayer meeting in the upper room. The sibling became a

---

[3] Jn.7:5

servant of his elder brother. As the years rolled by, he became the leader of the church in Jerusalem. The early church fathers record that he exercised a powerful preaching ministry with miraculous signs following. He was also a man of intense devotion, and it was said of him that his knees became so calloused from his constant kneeling before the Lord in prayer that they resembled camel's knees.

James was martyred. The early church fathers tell us that James, through his preaching, inadvertently alienated a lady called Piobsata from her husband, who just happened to be the Governor of Jerusalem. The incensed Governor stirred the Jews up against James, whereby they arrested him and threw him to his death from the Temple parapet. It would have been around AD62.

Going back to the young siblings growing up together, we can imagine that life together would have been at very close quarters. How could James not recognize that there was something different about his elder brother? I guess that you can live so close to the action that you don't actually see what is going on. Sometimes it takes a heavenly jolt to make us see who Jesus really is and what he is about. If we translate this into our daily lives together, it becomes quite a challenge. Do we recognize Christ in each other? Or are we so used to each other, with all our human faults, foibles, failures and weaknesses, that we do not recognise what God is doing in each other? May God open our eyes to see beyond the natural – as Paul would put it, not recognizing each other "according to the flesh" (2.Cor.5:16) – so that we might observe the life and work of Christ in each other.

Thought

The Bible teaches that "we have this treasure in jars of clay" (2.Cor.4:7). You, and your brothers and sisters in Christ, are all "jars of clay", and yet within, there is the life of Christ. Don't be caught up in seeing them in the natural. Can you see the life of Jesus within them?

Prayer

Dear Lord, I'm not sure how I would have handled having Jesus as my elder brother, growing up in our home. Help me, though, to begin to see him today within each of my spiritual brothers and sisters.

DAY TWO

Wherever You Are

1:1b (NLT)

I am writing to the "twelve tribes" – Jewish believers scattered abroad. Greetings!

This letter of James was written, not to any one individual, but to a very large group of people who were scattered all over the known world. The phrase is literally 'tais en tēi diasporā' – 'those in the dispersion'. These were the people of God who were living in faraway places other than the land of Israel. Three suggestions have been put forward by commentators as to exactly whom James was writing to.

The first suggestion is that he was writing to the millions of Jewish people who lived outside Palestine in Syria, Egypt, Greece, Rome – in fact all around the Mediterranean coastlands. Over the centuries, there had been three large movements of Hebrews: the first by the Assyrians around 722BC; then by the Babylonian King Nebuchadnezzar in 586BC; followed by Pompey in AD63 when he transported many Jews to Rome as slaves. During this time many thousands of Jews also left Palestine of their own choice, seeking better conditions in which to live and raise their families.

The second suggestion is that James was referring to the Christian Jews who lived away from the land of Israel. These would be Jews who had become Christians. In fact, James refers to them to them as those who "hold the faith in our Lord Jesus Christ". (2:1)

The third suggestion is that James was writing to the spiritual Israel – the Church of Jesus Christ. Paul, in his letter to the Galatian believers, refers to the church as "the Israel of God". (Gal.6:16) Paul also calls the church "the new man" which was in place of the two groups of

Jews and Gentiles. (Eph.2:15) Either the second or third suggestion makes more sense of the phrase "those in the Dispersion".

The actual word 'diasporā' is rich in meaning. It literally means 'to scatter or to sow abroad'. There is the strong thought that behind the 'scattering' is the missional purpose of God. There was a scattering that took place directly after the persecution of the church in Jerusalem, where it is recorded that after the execution of Stephen,

> ...there arose on that day a great persecution against the church in Jerusalem, and they were all scattered throughout the regions of Judea and Samaria, except the apostles.[4]

The Greek word translated 'scattered' is 'diaspeirō', which means 'to sow or scatter throughout'. It is intrinsically the same word. Luke further records that "those who were scattered went about preaching the word". (Acts 8:4) Here's a thought: in much the same way that the Lord Jesus spoke of the sower scattering the seed upon the ground, maybe that is what he is doing with us – scattering us into different places all over the world. And now we find ourselves rooted into a neighbourhood that has little or no idea of who Jesus is. We have been sown or planted there with a purpose. We then find a local church where we can worship with other believers and be nourished in our faith, and from which we reach out to those around us with the message of the kingdom of heaven. Maybe, just maybe, behind our move to where we now live, was the missional purpose of God. God wants his people everywhere, scattered as lights in the deep darkness, acting as salt in a corrupted world.

Here's another thought: wherever you are, the Word of God can come to you. Wherever we find ourselves today, and whatever we are going through, the Word of God can reach us. We are never out of his sight or out of his mind. Though we feel that we are far removed from the centre of spiritual activity, we are never out of range of his voice. His book, picked up and looked at with faith, can bring to us his life-giving word.

Thought

The Lord knows where he has placed us, and for what reason. His word can reach us wherever we are, and can nourish us in our faith.

---

[4]   Acts 8:1

Prayer

Lord, help me to see what you had in mind when you placed us here in our neighbourhood.

DAY THREE

Handling the Hard Times

1:2,3 (ESV)

Count it all joy, my brothers, when you meet trials of various kinds, for you know that the testing of your faith produces steadfastness.

These are probably some of the most quoted verses in the whole of the Bible. In them we find three things: undesired events, a desired reaction, and a divine purpose. Life can throw all sorts of things at us, most of them unsought. Here, James is talking about meeting or encountering various kinds of trials. The Greek word translated "meet" literally means 'to fall into something' or 'to have things fall around you'. Either way, suddenly you find yourself into something that was neither desired nor looked for. The word "trials" describes something that comes to you 'as a test or an experiment'. The Message describes them as "tests and challenges that come at you from all sides".

This is where we need to examine our biblical worldview. Are these trials the attempts of Satan to trip us up? Or are they the strategic workings of the Lord in order to develop, strengthen and mature our faith? Both can happen, and we need discernment to see what is actually going on. Often we are too quick to draw conclusions, and sometimes we think the trials are of the devil, and we resist them. James, however, was talking about the purposeful activity of God happening in the trials. Life, you see, is a school, and God uses the difficult stuff of life to teach us more about him, and more about ourselves.

James feels that when we fall into these difficult times that we ought to "count it all joy". One version[5] has it "pure joy". The Message version puts it like this: "Consider it a sheer gift..." The best paraphrase I have ever seen is that of J.B. Phillips, who writes:

> *When all kinds of trial and temptations crowd into your lives, my brothers, don't resent them as intruders, but welcome them as friends!*

This is a truly biblical worldview.

What, then, is behind all these un-pleasantries that fall around us? Simply this: they have arrived for the testing, revealing, strengthening and maturing of our faith. The Message version puts it this way:

> *You know that under pressure, your faith-life is forced into the open and shows its true colours.*

God will actually bring difficulties and pressures before us, and around us, to flush out the true nature of our faith. He does this because he wants our faith to be an 'approved' faith. In that light, then, because we are serious about the true quality of our faith, we are happier for him to bring it on.

Verse 3b in the English Standard Version says, "...the testing of your faith produces steadfastness." A key word for us to think about here is the word "produces". God's testing times are productive. The end result of such seasons of testing is "steadfastness" (ESV); "endurance" (NASB); "perseverance" (NIV). God is not interested in us having some 'flash in the pan' faith; he is more interested in developing us into men and women who have a 'long-haul' faith. These are the ones who have become what I would call 'seasoned warriors of faith', who have learned to interpret life as a training ground. In fact, the moment that we feel that we have learned all there is to know about this walk with the Lord, is when we have actually slipped into a delusion. This, then, is not a 'grit your teeth and press on' kind of attitude to life; this is a welcoming of the stretching and strengthening processes of God in our lives.

---

[5] NIV

Thought

Our attitudes and our responses to trials will tell the true story about the levels and the maturity of our faith. We cannot choose the circumstances, but we can choose our responses.

Prayer

Dear God, help me to see what you see when various trials hit my life. Help me to see from your perspective exactly what is going on, and then help me to respond in an appropriate manner.

DAY FOUR

Developing Maturity

1:4 (NLT)

*So let it grow, for when your endurance is fully developed,
you will be perfect and complete, needing nothing.*

Of all the strategists that I know of, God actually outshines them all, and his planning is very long term. The wonderful thing is that all of us, as individuals, are being fitted into his eternal purpose. God saw our place and our function in his church long before we ever opened our eyes into this world. He has a long-term plan for each one of us, and his desire is that we make the course, winning a crown at the end. That is why he schedules into our lives a series of training programmes that include things like trials and temptations.

Let's be clear on this: God uses all things to our benefit. The key to receiving the benefit, however, is our attitude toward whatever comes our way. And 'attitude' is instructed by 'understanding'. That's why we need to be constantly reading and meditating in the Scriptures in order to understand the ways, thoughts and purposes of God. And his ways, thoughts and purposes are totally different and higher to the ways, thoughts and purposes, however impressive, of this world. (Isa.55:8,9) If we react to the trials of life with frustration and anger, we can miss learning something, and we can forego the stretching and the strengthening of our faith.

When difficult times come upon us, falling around our ears, we must not seek to run from them. We must enter them with the knowledge that within them, there are precious things to find and learn. And when we are in them, we must not seek to cut and run from them. Eugene Peterson, in the Message, has it this way: "Don't try to get out of anything prematurely." Jesus, in the parable of the sower, talked about those who would 'do a runner' when trials came into their lives. He added the comment that they were not rooted well into the life of God. The word he used to describe them is the 'proskairoi' – the 'temporary, short-lived ones'. This walk with Christ was not meant to be a temporary and short-lived experience; it was designed to be far, far more than a lifelong experience.

So let the trial have its full effect. The Message puts it this way:

> *So don't try to get out of anything prematurely. Let it do its work so that you become mature and well developed, not deficient in any way.*

J.B. Phillips wrote it like this:

> *...but let the process go on until the endurance is fully developed, and you will find that you have become men of mature character with the right sort of independence.*

That actually is an interesting phrase: "the right sort of independence". What is he referring to? The Bible hints at it when Paul talks about becoming "content" in all things. (Phil.4:11) We will come to that later. The word "content" meant 'independent of outward circumstances'. True maturity is unmoved, un-influenced and unruffled by the outward circumstances of life. True maturity responds only to the movements and the whispers of God. That kind of maturity, however, doesn't come out of a textbook or even a solitary spiritual experience; it comes out of 'the school of the hard knocks'. This school is actually God's 'finishing school', where he is constantly at work, in and upon us, perfecting his handiwork in us. This is surely a privilege!

Thought

Living in a culture that finds difficulty with any form of long-term commitment, where will I be in my walk with Jesus in about twenty years from now?

Prayer

Dear Lord, put in me the heart of a long distance runner.

DAY FIVE

The Gaining of Wisdom

1:5-8 (ESV)

If any of you lacks wisdom, let him ask God, who gives generously to all without reproach, and it will be given him. But let him ask in faith, with no doubting, for the one who doubts is like a wave of the sea that is driven and tossed by the wind. For that person must not suppose that he will receive anything from the Lord; he is a double-minded man, unstable in all his ways.

There is a great difference between wisdom and its counterpart, knowledge. Knowledge will tell you what we need to know, whereas wisdom will tell you what to do with, and how to handle, that knowledge. I remember hearing the late John Wimber say:

Knowledge will tell you that there is a bull in a china shop; wisdom will tell you how to get it out without breaking a cup!

In this respect, wisdom is a doing word. Furthermore, biblical wisdom is more a matter of the heart than the head. A wise person is not necessarily a clever person.

It is no crime to admit that in certain circumstances we do not know what to do. In fact, humility demands that we own up quickly to the fact that we are not the fount of all knowledge and wisdom in all things! Blessed is the man who says he doesn't know what to do, but that he knows One who does. James goes on to say that God is a generous giver of wisdom. We are encouraged to come 'to the giving God' (literal translation). Out of interest also, I looked up the word "generously" and found that it is the Greek word 'haplous', which occurs in this form only here. It literally means 'simply'. In other words, there are no hidden clauses, no hidden agendas; it is simply and easily given.

This next phrase is so releasing. James says that God gives wisdom to all "without reproach". He doesn't sit there thinking how stupid we are! In fact, it's quite the opposite; he delights that we ask. The Preacher's Commentary adds:

> It is not only God's character to give generously; it is also His character to build us up. He does not wish to tear us down. Indeed, He neither refuses nor reproaches anyone; He never puts anyone down. He is the Master Builder.[6]

I do think, however, that sometimes he watches and winces whenever we strike out on our own, without any reference to him, thinking that we are more than capable of resolving anything that life throws at us.

James gives us only one prerequisite for obtaining the wisdom of God, and it is that of faith. This is not faith in the existence of God; rather, it is faith in the fact that he loves to give to those who ask. He then enlarges on that faith by adding "with no doubting". There should be no hesitancy in approaching him and there should be no self-doubts (i.e. am I worthy? will he listen to me? will he think that I am stupid?) We are encouraged to approach confidently as a child of God, as a son would to a gracious father. This, of course, throws up the whole issue of having a healthy view of God as our Father. This has to be right. If it isn't, if we do doubt him, if we do question his love and generosity, then we shall be like the waves of the sea that are "driven" and "tossed" by the wind. We shall be at the mercy of circumstances, the latest opinions and the strongest characters.

"Let's see how he handles this," said the father to himself as he introduced his son to an area of life that he had never tackled before. The lad looked at it all with apprehension, and the father noticed the look in his eye. "I'll be here," he said. "Just ask if you need any help."

Thought

The landscape of life is littered with the wreckage of projects and schemes that have been attempted for God with little or no reference

---

[6] *The Preachers Commentary*, commenting on Jas.1:5 – e-sword.net

to him. Better to get close to him, to listen to him, and obey his promptings, than run at the world with a clutch of good ideas.

Prayer

Lord, help me to be aware and comfortable with my own limitations. May they teach me to look to you more and more.

DAY SIX

Spiritual Instability

Yesterday, we looked at God's generosity when it comes to the obtaining of wisdom. James Motyer writes, "God's unclouded desire for our spiritual progress ... can be summed up in three words: simplicity, availability, liberality."[7] And as John Bunyan would say, "He giveth without twittering."

Today, I want us to stay with this thought about the person who doubts. The word here is not so much stark unbelief, but the inability to choose between faith and unbelief. It rightly describes an individual faced with two or more decisions, and unable to make the right one. Vincent's Word Studies says that the word is "not equivalent to unbelief, but expresses the hesitation which balances between faith and unbelief, and inclines toward the latter"[8]. In other words, and in this case, the individual is unsure about the Father's love and the Father's generosity, saying in effect, "I'm not sure that he loves me, and I'm not sure that I am welcome in his presence with all my anxieties and questions. I don't want to bother him." Such a view of God grieves the Father. I try to imagine my five children carrying those kinds of thoughts in their heart.

There are spiritual consequences to this kind of ambivalence. Unable to be settled on this fundamental issue of the love and simple generosity of our Father in heaven, we find that we are unsettled on most things in life. We are described as "a wave driven and tossed about by the wind". This phrase is found only here in the New Testament. It describes a wave that is tossed high, driven down, spun round and round, and generally makes very little progress. In like

---

[7]   J. A. Motyer, *The Message of James: The Tests of Faith*, (IVP, London, 1970), p.44
[8]   *Vincent's Word Studies*, e-sword.net

manner, such a person is always in a state of inward agitation, indecisive, vacillating and generally unstable, and makes very little progress in their spiritual walk. They are characterised by indecision and uncertainty. John Bunyan actually calls this individual 'Mr. Facing-both-ways'. The prophet Elijah also accused Israel of "limping" between two opinions. (1.Kgs.18:21)

James goes on to call this state of affairs "double-mindedness", or more literally 'two-souled'. This is another word that is used only here and in Jas.4:8. The Weymouth translation of the NT puts it this way:

> Such a one is a man of two minds, undecided in every step he takes.

This describes someone who prays because they are anxious, and then goes out and acts as though they had never prayed in the first place! This also describes the one who prays and then keeps all their options open. This kind of walk ensures that one will not receive anything at all from the Lord. Heaven will simply shut its doors.

Spiritual stability is profoundly grounded in the love of God our Father, and has as its roots a deep awareness of his generous heart. So when God, in his loving mentoring of our lives, brings us to situations that are beyond our natural ability to resolve, our response should be that of a child happily reaching for his hand, knowing full well that we are loved, appreciated and cherished. That is a very stable relationship that will go far.

Thought

Insecurity in any relationship is never constructive; it is always damaging. How secure are you in God's love? Do you know in your heart that he loves you?

Prayer

Father, help me to relax into your love for me today, knowing that whatever I feel about myself, you are always looking out for me, and ready to help me when I call to you.

DAY SEVEN

A Temporary View of Life (I)

1:9-11 (NLT)

Believers who are poor have something to boast about, for God has honored them. And those who are rich should boast that God has humbled them. They will fade away like a little flower in the field. The hot sun rises and the grass withers; the little flower droops and falls, and its beauty fades away. In the same way, the rich will fade away with all of their achievements.

The little phrase 'nothing lasts forever' has both a positive and a negative feel to it. In this next section of the letter, James is contrasting those who are desperately poor and those who are rich, and he is speaking in the literal sense of the words. Here, he is describing two groups of people, who are seemingly poles apart, and he is expressing how each group should think about how they find themselves, and what their attitudes should be.

Imagine James in the familiar setting of the hills surrounding Bethlehem. H.B. Tristam, in his 'Natural History of the Bible' (1868) wrote:

> *The downs of Bethlehem in February are one spangled carpet of brilliant flowers ... in May all traces of verdure are gone.*[9]

Nothing lasts forever.

---

[9] H.B. Tristram, *Natural History of the Bible*, (1868), cited by James Adamson, *The Epistle of James*, The New International Commentary on the New Testament series, (Eerdmans, Michigan, 1976), p.63

James first addresses the poor man. He calls him "the lowly brother". It literally reads, '…the brother, the lowly one.' This is not a condition to be spiritualized; this is an actual condition.

Barnes puts it this way:

> [It] means one in humble circumstances; one of lowly rank or employment; one in a condition of dependence or poverty.[10]

The society of the day disregarded such people to the extent that it was felt that they should be driven out of the land. James is saying to this humble brother that although society looks down on him, he is actually to adopt a high view of himself. The apostle Paul wrote of Jesus:

> …for you know the grace of our Lord Jesus Christ, that though he was rich, yet for your sake he became poor, so that you by his poverty might become rich.[11]

In the eyes of the Jesus who "though he was rich … became poor", there are incredible benefits from such a state of living. James Adamson in his wonderful commentary on James talks about the "the richness of humble circumstances"[12].

We do well to remember that poverty was a state that Jesus himself chose, so there is the strong sense of identification with those he came to save. The good news was to be preached to the poor. Among the lowly brothers, there is a richness of faith to be found now, and the promise of riches in heaven to be enjoyed later. James would write a little later in his letter:

> Listen, my beloved brothers, has not God chosen those who are poor in the world to be rich in faith and heirs of the kingdom, which he has promised to those who love him?[13]

I want to suggest that, where there are many options, many avenues of provision, faith will struggle, whereas on the other hand, where there

---

[10] Albert Barnes, *Notes on the Bible*, e-sword.net
[11] 2.Cor.8:9
[12] James Adamson, *The Epistle of James*, The New International Commentary on the New Testament series, (Eerdmans, Michigan, 1976)
[13] Jas.2:5

are no more options and no more avenues, faith is often thrown in the deep end and learns to swim.

Nothing lasts forever. The lowly brother will not remain forever in that state. In fact, he is to see and boast in his exaltation. God highly regards him, even if society disregards him. In God's eyes, he is a prince among men, a strong warrior of faith, and one who has an incredible treasure waiting for him in the next life. Mary the mother of Jesus cried out in the Spirit, "...he has filled the hungry with good things, and the rich he has sent away empty." (Lk.1:53)

Thought

Jesus taught that our attitude to the least of his brethren actually reflects our attitude towards the Lord himself. (Matt.25:40)

Prayer

Dear Lord Jesus, help me to look upon the poor of this world with your eyes, and to treat them with the same due respect that you do.

DAY EIGHT

A Temporary View of Life (II)

D o not let anybody tell you that being rich is thoroughly wrong and sinful. Rather, it is more often than not the result of the blessing of God upon the industrious and hard-working individual. Both aspects are seen to be working in tandem. According to the book of Proverbs, poverty usually comes to the lazy, whereas wealth and prosperity usually come to the diligent. What the Bible is more concerned about, however, is how you get rich and what you do with your riches.

In this passage, we are talking about the temporariness of the things of life. Yesterday we looked at the temporary state of the lowly man, and how he should view himself. Today, we look at his counterpart, the rich man, and we will seek to learn how he should view himself and his state in life. James comes to the point quickly: "Let the rich brother boast in his humiliation." This is a good rendering of the meaning of the text. The man who is rich, who is also a Christian, has, or ought to have, a kingdom view of his treasures. J.B. Mayor, in his commentary on this letter, says that this is "the intrinsic effect of Christianity in changing our view of life"[14].

James Adamson calls this little section "the potential poverty of riches". The wealthy Christian, who has a truly kingdom view of life, has seen through the temporariness of his wealth, and views it as something that could be 'here today and gone tomorrow'. He has learned with the psalmist:

---

[14] J.B. Mayor, *The Epistle of St James,* cited by James Adamson, *The Epistle of James*, The New International Commentary on the New Testament series, (Eerdmans, Michigan, 1976), p.62

If riches increase, set not your heart on them.[15]

He has also observed the wisdom of Proverbs:

Do not toil to acquire wealth; be discerning enough to desist. When your eyes light on it, it is gone, for suddenly it sprouts wings, flying like an eagle toward heaven.[16]

He has also understood the words of Jesus:

Take care, and be on your guard against all covetousness, for one's life does not consist in the abundance of his possessions.[17]

James says that the rich man is to "boast … in his humiliation". This is interesting, because here we have a play on words going on. There is the brother who is lowly ('tapeinos') and the brother who makes himself lowly ('tapeinosis'). In this way, both brothers are sharing the values and the attitudes of the kingdom.

How then should we view wealth? Bearing in mind that Jesus talked about the "deceitfulness" of riches (Mk.4:19), and that "[our] life does not consist in the abundance of our possessions" and that we should not lay up treasure for ourselves (Lk.12:21), a biblical view of wealth is that it is both useful and seductive. Paul wrote to Timothy:

For the love of money is a root of all kinds of evils. It is through this craving that some have wandered away from the faith and pierced themselves with many pangs.[18]

Money in itself is not evil; it is the love of money that can lead to evil. To keep it 'clean', therefore, it should be generated and used with others in mind. Let the rich man glory, then, in his identification with the Saviour who "though he was rich, yet for your sake he became poor, so that you by his poverty might become rich". (2.Cor.8:9) Temporal wealth that is accumulated for its own sake turns into dust, but when it is sown into the kingdom, it is transformed into eternal wealth.

---

[15] Psa.62:10b
[16] Prov.23:4,5
[17] Lk.12:15
[18] 1.Tim.6:10

Thought

Our attitude towards money and possessions is a good litmus test of whether or not, in God's sight, we are rich or poor. We either hold them tightly or lightly.

Prayer

Grant me, dear Lord, to see that whatever I own or possess, it is actually held by me in trust. Grant me the joy of being a good steward of your good gifts.

DAY NINE

A Temporary View of Life (III)

An old and familiar story is often told of a very rich Christian who died and went to heaven. When she arrived at the gates, she asked to be shown at once to her mansion. Peter, keeping quiet, accompanied her. As they walked into paradise, she noticed a magnificent mansion set back in lush grounds. "Is that mine?" she demanded. Peter shook his head, and beckoned her to move on. They then passed another mansion, not quite so magnificent, and again the question was asked, "Is that mine?" Peter shook his head and nudged her forward. On and on they went, and as they travelled, the houses decreased in size. At the end of the road, they came to a wooden shed. "That's yours," said Peter sadly. The woman exploded with rage, and then asked to whom the first mansion they had seen belonged. "That belongs to Miss Ethel Hampstead who used to live in Brighton." The woman responded, "I know her! She never had two pennies to rub together all her life!" "I know," said Peter, "but the money she sent up was enough to build this place with."

A wealthy unbeliever, speaking of his friend who was a poor Christian, said, "When I die, I shall leave my riches. When he dies, he will go to his."[19]

A good balance is found in the words of Agur, son of Jakeh, encapsulated in the book of Proverbs. He wrote:

Two things I ask of you; deny them not to me before I die:
Remove far from me falsehood and lying; give me neither
poverty nor riches; feed me with the food that is needful for

---

[19]   James Adamson, *The Epistle of James*, The New International Commentary on the New Testament series, (Eerdmans, Michigan, 1976), p.66

me, lest I be full and deny you and say, "Who is the LORD?" or lest I be poor and steal and profane the name of my God.[20]

Remember the words of J.B. Mayor as he described the hills of Bethlehem which "in February are one spangled carpet of brilliant flowers"[21], and yet a few months later, there is no trace of them. James would recall all this as he wrote these words. The scorching winds had reduced them to nothing. If we lived in Palestine, we would encounter 'the sirocco', which is a blasting, scorching southeast wind which howls through there in the spring. Once it starts, it is incessant both night and day. James gives a reason why these two groups of people – the lowly poor and the rich – should adapt this kingdom attitude and mindset; it is because there is a transience about their states. James concentrates here, though, on the transient beauty of the wealthy man. He writes, "Its flower falls, and its beauty perishes." The word translated "flower" is better 'blossom' and the word translated "beauty" speaks of the superficial and transient face of the flower. It is literally 'of the face of it'. The beautiful rose is pitiful when withered.

What is James teaching us here? I think he is showing us how to be rich and also how to be poor. The key word is contentment. The person who is truly rich is the person who has learned to be content. There is no clamouring here, either for a release from being poor, or to get in on a race to get rich. James put the whole issue firmly in its place. In whatever state you find yourself, seek first the way of the kingdom and be at peace in yourself.

Thought

Jesus said, "Where your treasure is, there your heart will be also." (Matt.6:21) The Preacher's Commentary says, "Gathering earthly treasures is not a great enough cause by which to structure a philosophy of life."[22]

---

[20] Prov.30:8,9
[21] H.B. Tristram, *Natural History of the Bible*, (1868), cited by James Adamson, *The Epistle of James*, The New International Commentary on the New Testament series, (Eerdmans, Michigan, 1976), p.63
[22] *The Preacher's Commentary*, commenting on Matt.6:21, e-sword.net

Prayer

Dear God, take from my heart both greed and resentment. Both give me unhealthy heartache.

DAY TEN

Sticking It Out

1:12 (ESV)

Blessed is the man who remains steadfast under trial, for when he has stood the test he will receive the crown of life, which God has promised to those who love him.

James now brings us back to this issue of facing trials. He has made us look at two areas: namely, how to handle the lack of wisdom and how to handle money.

The word "trial" is a very generic word – it can mean a whole raft of things. Earlier, James talked about "various trials", meaning that they can come in all shapes and sizes. They can come in the form of a sickness, a financial crisis, circumstantial pressures, the working of the enemy in opposition or in temptation. What is clear is that the Christian is not immune to them; in fact, they come to mature us and to strengthen our faith. Sin and sinful ways are so deeply ingrained in us that it takes the fire of a furnace to draw it out. Trials come, therefore, to purify our inner life.

Trials also come to test the authenticity and reality of our faith. They provoke questions within us such as, "Does God care about me?" "Is God all powerful?" "Is what he says true?" In each one of them, our faith is called into question and then into action. And each time we exercise our faith, it grows a little more.

We are to think discerningly of these trials. In all instances, we are to think of them, not as a race where only one wins, but as an examination where all have the possibility of passing. We are to think of some of these trials as friends who can help us, rather than enemies who come to defeat us. We are to think of others as the powers of darkness that seek to distract and defeat us. We need to respond carefully, thoughtfully and prayerfully to each and every one of them. Whatever they are, however, James tell us to "count it all joy" when they turn up on our door. Matthew Henry wrote in his commentary:

> Philosophy may instruct men to be calm under their troubles; but Christianity teaches them to be joyful...

James commends the one who "remains steadfast", who 'stands the test'. The temptations to handle the trial badly are numerous: we can get disgruntled and moan; we can allow ourselves to get depressed; we can kick out in anger and resentment. All these are negative responses to trials, and they can all lead to sin in one way or another. Peterson puts it like this in the Message:

> Anyone who meets a testing challenge head-on and manages to stick it out is mighty fortunate.

To remain steadfast and to stand the test meets with approval. No one will trust anything or anyone who is untested. They both meet with disapproval. Both are unapproved. God's intention for our lives is that we become the approved ones, the ones who have walked through the trials that both life and the devil throw at us almost unrelentingly, and have come out stronger for it. Remember, we can never be a victor if we have never faced a battle. God's desire is that the strength of our faith is mature and mighty. A tried man or woman is of great proven value in the kingdom of God.

Thought

Trials and temptations are there, not to strip our faith, but to strengthen our faith.

Prayer

Dear Lord, please help me to welcome and submit myself to your faith-enhancing activities that come my way through the trials and temptations of life.

DAY ELEVEN

Understanding Temptation (I)

1:13-15 (NLT)

And remember, when you are being tempted, do not say, "God is tempting me." God is never tempted to do wrong and he never tempts anyone else. Temptation comes from our own desires, which entice us and drag us away. These desires give birth to sinful actions. And when sin is allowed to grow, it gives birth to death.

I love words. They can be so rich in meaning and they can be very powerful in their effect. God chooses to use them. This word "tempted" is the Greek word 'peirazō', and it is a big word and an interesting word. The word translated "temptation" is 'peirasmos', and it is generic in that it spawns a huge variety of meanings. It can be translated 'trials', 'temptations', 'tests', 'challenges', 'adversities', 'afflictions'. James Adamson, in his commentary, writes:

> *The noun appears about four times in secular Greek, with meanings varying from doctors' experiments with drugs to 'general ills'.[23]*

The root meaning of the word is 'to test or to put to the proof'.

There is genius in the way James puts this together. Firstly, he treats the source of the temptation – let's use that word here, and this is a big subject. Bear in mind that we have already said that we must be discerning here. There is a 'peirasmos' that comes to purify, sharpen

---

[23] James Adamson, *The Epistle of James*, The New International Commentary on the New Testament series, (Eerdmans, Michigan, 1976), p.28

and mature us, and there is also a 'peirasmos' that comes to oppose us, to distract us and throw us off track. Both test the strength of our faith. And both are to be received with joy – the joy of going through the process of being matured and strengthened, and also the joy of being proved and tried in battle.

Adamson writes:

> *Welcome peirasmos; it consummates discipleship by forcing you to exercise in practice what you have learned in Christ.*[24]

The Preacher's Commentary says:

> *In other words, temptation can be used for our good or for our harm. The outcome depends upon our response to the temptation.*[25]

Temptations do not come from God. The structure of the Greek language makes it clear that God is not the source of our temptations or our trials. I want to suggest that there is a certain neutrality about 'peirasmos'. A trial can be used by God or by the devil. God is not the source of them – they are all out there as a result of the Fall – but he can and he does use them for our benefit.

One thing we need to understand about God is that he cannot be tempted. Barnes writes (and here I abbreviate):

> *There is no evil passion [in God] to be gratified, as there is in men; there is no want of power; ... no want of wealth, ... [and] no want of happiness.*[26]

He is complete in himself, and evil simply has no attraction to him at all.

When it comes, then, to the question of who is to blame, we can safely say that the blame culture is as old as the hills. Adam blamed both Eve (directly) and God (indirectly) for his failure to keep the commandment, and Eve blamed the devil. Incidentally, it was Flip Wilson, the American comedian, who made popular the phrase, 'The devil made me do it.' The bottom line is that the real blame is to be found from within ourselves. As Peterson writes in the Message, "The temptation to give in to evil comes from us and only us." In order to

---

[24] Ibid, p.15
[25] *The Preacher's Commentary*, commenting on Jas.1:13, e-sword.net
[26] Albert Barnes, *Notes on the Bible*, commenting on Jas.1:13, e-sword.net

make real spiritual progress, we must learn to take personal responsibility for our choices in life. When things go wrong, the immaturity in us wants to find someone else to blame; maturity, however, takes it on the chin and owns up and says, "It was my fault." The words 'forgive me' are far better.

Thought

Falling into temptation is never an isolated act. It has a background in our hearts...[27]

Prayer

Help me, Lord, to recognize that when the temptation to sin comes, it comes recognizing the weaknesses and the proneness of my own heart. Please make me more honest with myself.

---

[27] J.A. Motyer, *The Message of James: The Tests of Faith*, (IVP, London, 1970), p.29

Day Twelve

Understanding Temptation (II)

I t's a lot easier to tackle something when you understand what is going on. That is why we are spending a little time around this whole area of understanding temptation, or trials. Because we live in a fallen world, where there is so much that is systemically wrong, it is no wonder that we come up against trials and temptations. But it is how we discern and handle them that shapes our stories.

James is very clear that God cannot be tempted, and tempts no-one, laying the reason for our temptations right at our door. He says that "each person is tempted when he is lured and enticed by his own desire". Peterson puts it even more bluntly in the Message:

> *The temptation to give in to evil comes from us and only us. We have no one to blame but the leering, seducing flare-up of our own lust.*

How does it happen? There are two words that are used here that are important to understand. The first is "lured" (ESV), "carried away" (NASB), "dragged away" (NIV). The Greek word is 'exelkō' which means 'to draw away out of'. It speaks of an animal, a fish or even a person who is drawn or lured out of a place of safety and security. It is being persuaded and given a sense that there is no danger. The second word is "enticed" (ESV/NASB/NIV). The Greek word is 'deleazō' which means 'taken with a bait'. This phrase is in the middle voice, and clearly gives the sense of passively allowing oneself to be enticed. Again and again, the choice comes back to us. No one makes a fish jump on to a baited hook. If we have been 'hooked' or 'caught', it was because we allowed it to happen. If we were more aware that our adversary, the devil, is prowling around like a lion seeking someone to trap and devour, then we would walk more carefully through life. Satan is a skilful fisherman, a very clever trapper.

What is it, then, that entices us? A better question is, what is it in us that entices us? The drag, the pull towards sin is definitely from within us. The outward temptation appeals to something deep within all of us. Someone rightly said, "If temptation struck no responsive chord, it would not be temptation." We are lured and enticed by our own desire. According to Scripture, all of us are attracted by "the desires of the flesh and the desires of the eyes and pride in possessions" (1.Jn.2:16). Even the godly warrior King David got caught. He was in the wrong place at the wrong time, and he saw something which he then allowed to feed his imagination. That resulted in him embarking on a sudden slide into adultery and murder. His salvation came as a result of his personal 'mia culpa' – 'I have sinned'.

Kenneth Wuest, a wonderful Bible commentator, wrote concerning the sinful nature:

> [It] is an intangible, invisible entity, and cannot be watched. It is an unseen enemy whose tactics cannot be observed and therefore cannot be guarded against. But the saint is able to keep watch over the members of his body, what his eyes look at, his ears listen to, his mind thinks about, his hands do, and where his feet carry him.[28]

Let us be aware that within each of us, there resides still an untamed and restless evil, however much we cover it up and seek to subdue it. Blessed is that man or woman who is aware of the natural bent towards sin that lives within. It keeps us humble and very dependent upon his grace, thankful for his mercy and patience and determined for mutual accountability.

Thought

"Within me is both a dove and a wolf," said the young novice monk to the desert Father. "I am afraid the wolf will win. What shall I do?" The wise Father replied, "Feed the one and starve the other."

---

[28] Kenneth S. Wuest, *Romans, Word Studies in the Greek New Testament, Vol.1,* (Eerdmans, Michigan, 1973), p.107

Prayer

Dear God, fan within me both a love for the holy, and a hatred for the evil.

DAY THIRTEEN

Understanding Temptation (III)

We are staying one more day on this whole subject of temptation. The main reason for this is because church life is tragically full of people who have succumbed to temptation in one way or another, and have 'fallen by the wayside'. We need to be aware that there is an enemy out there who is actively seeking to trip us up and to knock us out of the purposes of God for our lives. And he knows exactly where to aim and lay his bait. He sees something within us – an inbuilt propensity to sin.

The key word in all this is desire. The word is 'epithumia' and it means 'a desire, a craving, a passion, a longing, a desire for what is forbidden, lust'. Be assured about this: it is inbuilt. We got it from our father Adam, and if left unchecked and undealt with, it will take us not only to the grave, but also into a Christ-less eternity. Even as Christians, we find that it still wants to raise its ugly head, and Satan knows how to hunt for our weak spots.

As we look at this text, we find that there is a definite progression taking place. There is conception, birth, fully grown and then death. Peterson captures it like this:

> *Lust gets pregnant, and has a baby: sin! Sin grows up to adulthood, and becomes a real killer.*[29]

All desires have a growth gene within them.

Let's unpack this a little. As we look at this progression, we can see that the desire comes before sin. Temptation is not sin; it is the giving into temptation that is sin. This, then, is where we need to begin, by looking at the desires. And then we will find that at the back of the desires are our thoughts. This is where it all starts. First a thought...

---

[29] The Message

I want to quote at this point at length a passage from the little but powerful book, 'The Imitation of Christ' by Thomas à Kempis. He writes:

> *Above all, we must be especially alert against the beginnings of temptation, for the enemy is more easily conquered if he is refused admittance to the mind and is met beyond the threshold when he knocks. Someone has said very aptly: "Resist the beginnings; remedies come too late, when by long delay the evil has gained strength." First, a mere thought comes to mind, then strong imagination, followed by pleasure, evil delight, and consent. Thus, because he is not resisted in the beginning, Satan gains full entry. And the longer a man delays in resisting, so much the weaker does he become each day, while the strength of the enemy grows against him.[30]*

All spiritual masters are agreed in this: the battle starts in the mind. First a thought… and left unchecked and unchallenged, it will wreak havoc within. Pope Gregory (AD 600) said in a letter to Augustine, the missionary to England:

> *All sin occurs in three ways, that is, by suggestion, pleasure, and consent. Suggestion through the devil, pleasure through the body, and consent through the will.[31]*

We do, however, have the choice in these matters. If we wait until the desires have conceived within us, we will find it difficult to resist. But if we determine to bring every thought captive to the obedience of Christ as soon as they appear, then we will find that we will be winning the battle. So, let's stop looking for someone or something to blame; let's start to fight back in Jesus' name!

Thought

Either my thoughts will capture me, or I will capture my thoughts. (2.Cor.10:4-6)

---

[30] Thomas à Kempis, *The Imitation of Christ*, Book 1 (Hendrickson Publishers, Massachusetts, 2004), p.13
[31] Gregory the Great, *Registrum Epistolarum*, Book XI, Letter 64, retrieved from http://www.newadvent.org/fathers/360211064.htm

Prayer

Jesus, I can't stop the thoughts entering my head, but I can stop them in your name before they wind their way into my feelings and choices. Help me to be more alert to their knockings on the door of my mind.

DAY FOURTEEN

Do Not Be Deceived

1:16 (NLT)

So don't be misled, my dear brothers and sisters.

This verse before us is what we call a 'transition' verse or a 'bridging' verse – in other words, it comes between two lines of thought. James was not a tidy writer; he didn't "organize his material into specific paragraphs"[32]. There are two streams of thought that are connected here by this verse. The first is that we are subject to trials and temptations, and the second is that God is a source of all goodness. The first is that Satan deceives and the second is that God speaks the truth.

We must not forget, however, that the root of sin lies within ourselves. Matthew Henry wrote:

> *We are the authors and procurers of all sin and misery to ourselves ... God is not, cannot be, the author and patronizer of any thing that is evil; but must be acknowledged as the cause and spring of every thing that is good.[33]*

In respect to it all beginning with our thoughts, I found another translation of Thomas à Kempis on this:

> *At first it is a mere thought confronting the mind; then the imagination paints it in stronger colours; only after that do*

---

[32] *The Preacher's Commentary*, commenting on Jas.1:16, e-sword.net
[33] Matthew Henry, *Commentary on the Whole Bible*, commenting on Jas.1:14, e-sword.net

46

*we take pleasure in it, and the will makes a false move, and
we give our assent.*[34]

James tells us not to be deceived. Deception is Satan's master plan. Eve got it right in the garden when she said, "The serpent deceived me." The word translated "deceived" can mean 'to be led astray, to be caused to roam and to wander'. It builds up a picture of being taken off the main road, down some beaten track where certain dangers await us. It gives the sense that Satan wants to have us off target, without focus and directionless, ending up in a wasteland. The verb is a present passive, and so it means can be translated, "Do not allow yourselves to be deceived." It means that we can *allow* ourselves to be led astray; it isn't forced upon us.

On another tack, the genius of a clever deception is that it looks so much like the real thing. The bait on the hook looks genuine. The power of deception is that it awakens desires within us, opening up colourful vistas, feeding our imagination, promising so much. When we get wise to it, however, we realize that the gratification is sudden and quickly gone, leaving a bad taste in the mouth and a conscience riddled with guilt.

So, we should not be deceived about the source of temptation and sin. It lies within us, and is inflamed by an enemy who wishes to throw us off track into the wilderness. And we should not be deceived about the source of all goodness and truth. It is God. The Preacher's Commentary says:

> *He is not only the source of good, but He is the One who is
> committed to making all things work together for good for
> His children, those who are called according to His
> purpose.*[35]

Our human nature is so bent out of shape, and Satan loves to twist things around, but God is straight and true, and he will build those qualities into us as we walk in trust with him.

---

[34] Thomas à Kempis, *The Imitation of Christ*, Book 1, translated by Ronald Knox, (Burns and Oates, London, 1959), p.43

[35] *The Preacher's Commentary,* commenting on Jas.1:17, e-sword.net

Thought

Under God's hands, the 'bent out of shape' can be reshaped, and can learn to walk straight.

Prayer

Oh Lord, thank you that you have not left me to hobble through life in the best way that I can. Your touch can straighten me up, and I can walk day by day, leaning on you, and we will get there!

DAY FIFTEEN

The Reliable God

1:17 (ESV)

Every good gift and every perfect gift is from above, coming down from the Father of lights, with whom there is no variation or shadow due to change.

We now begin to focus on what God is like. He is the source of all that is good, his Word is truth, and he is thoroughly reliable. Having painted a picture of how sin distorts and brings us to death, we now begin to see how exposure to the One who said, "I am the way, the truth and the life," can straighten up our bent and twisted lives and bring us into life. Satan's words are 'death' words; God's words are 'life' words.

Just a little digging reveals that the two words translated "gift" are not the same words in the original language. The first is 'dosis', and the second is 'dōrēma'. They are different in that the first refers to the act of giving, or the gift in its initiatory stage; the second refers to the thing given, a boon when perfected. The first, if you like, is the 'shoot'; the second is the 'fruit'. There seems to be a contrasting going on here to the growing and infiltrating work of sin.

There is firstly the initiating stage of conception, and then there is the concluding stage of death. That which sin starts and finishes leads us to death. That which God starts and finishes leads us to life; and be assured, whatever God starts, he finishes.

I am reminded of the words of Paul to the Philippian believers:

And I am sure of this, that he who began a good work in you will bring it to completion at the day of Jesus Christ.[36]

We now come to a lovely description of God himself. He is called, literally, 'the Father of the lights'. This phrase is only found here in the whole of the New Testament. The word "Father" is used in the Hebrew sense of being the One who is the source of all things. God is the Father, the Source of all light, ranging from that first divine light that shone into the darkness of the early creation to the One who set all the lights in the sky – some to give light, and others to reflect light. And as the sun in our own galaxy gives light, so we, like the moon, are designed to reflect that light. God shines; we reflect. He is the One who would shed light into the darkness of our hearts. His Son said of himself that he was the light of the world, the One who would dispel the darkness of the world that had enfolded our hearts. We are encouraged to walk in this light, with him and also with each other. As we live in him, we find ourselves then, firstly as individuals, and then more fully as a body of believers, becoming the light of the world.

Whereas the ways of evil twist and turn, causing distortions and shadows in our lives, there is absolutely none of that with God. The word "variation" is 'parallagē', and it means among other things 'to be fickle'. God is not fickle. Just as the earth consistently orbits around the unchanging sun, and yet each year is different, so as we live in and around God, we will find a strong constancy about him that will want to affect our lives. The phrase "shadow due to change" can be literally read as 'shadow-mark'. The natural lights leave shadow-marks. Shadows come from where the light does not touch. On the other hand, whenever and wherever God shines into our lives, there will be no shadows. His light is a constant, probing, healing and restorative light. Living in the light of God is the best place to be.

Light dawns in the darkness for the upright; gracious, merciful, and righteous.[37]

God is our constant in life. He is not subject to mood swings or vacillations. We can take our bearings from him. He has a purpose for us, and he will not be distracted from it. He is faithful even when we are not.

---

[36] Phil.1:6
[37] Psa.112:4 (lit.)

Thought

If it were down to our grip on God, we would quickly fall. Thankfully, his grip on us is stronger. (Psa.37:23,24/Psa.138:8)

Prayer

Dear God, at times I feel that I am all over the place. Help me to rest today in the firmness of your plans and purpose for my life.

DAY SIXTEEN

The Best Gift

1:18 (ESV)

Of his own will he brought us forth by the word of truth, that we should be a kind of firstfruits of his creatures.

God is a great giver, and everything that he gives to us is good. All this giving is set in the context of the one who is unwavering in his goodness. God will not change from this. He is absolutely trustworthy, and he only gives us good gifts.

The greatest gift that he gave to us was the gift of salvation. Even when we were torn and damaged, warped and twisted, tainted and tarnished by sin and evil, he reached down to us in mercy and rescued us. He gave us the good gifts of forgiveness, of cleansing, and of adoption into his family.

James tells us, "Of His own will, he brought us forth by the word of truth." The NASB translates it, "In the exercise of his will..." The Preacher's Commentary notes:

> *One of the great mysteries of theology is the tender balance between the sovereignty of God and the free will of man. James reminds us here in this verse of the fact that God initiated our salvation by His own will. Without a doubt, He is the aggressive lover; He is the initiator; He is the One who loved us while we were yet His enemies.[38]*

We are reminded of the verse in John's Gospel which reads:

> *But to all who did receive him, who believed in his name, he gave the right to become children of God, who were born,*

---

[38] *The Preacher's Commentary*, commenting on Jas.1:18, e-sword.net

not of blood, nor of the will of the flesh, nor of the will of man, but of God.[39]

The good gift of salvation came from the Father, and it came from above.

The result of this saving work of God was that we were born again. The Greek word translated "brought us forth" is 'apokueō', which means 'to bring forth from the womb', literally 'gave birth to us'. This is firmly in line with something else that Jesus said, recorded for us in the Gospel of John. He said to Nicodemus, "Unless one is born again, he cannot see the kingdom of God." (Jn.3:3) That literally reads, 'Unless one is born from above…' Our new birth didn't come from us, or originate with us, or from around us; it came from heaven, and it was a gift from the Father. One of my first mentors in the faith said to me, "The fact that you thank God for your salvation shows that he is responsible for it."

The means of this salvation was "the word of truth", or more literally, 'a word of truth'. What is this word that we hear that has so much creative power within us? The thought is this: just one word of truth from God, sown into our lives, has such regenerative and creative power that our lives cannot contain it; the word is larger than us. Bob Mumford speaks of the effect of receiving this salvation word from God, comparing it as feeling like a mouse which has been impregnated by elephant seed!

We become the firstfruits of his creatures. The Greek word translated "firstfruits" is 'aparchē', which means 'first in order of time', but also carries a sense of something of more excellence. Because of what God has given to us, and sown into us, we are not 'mere men and women'. Something of heaven has been put into our souls, and we can never be the same again. Human desire gives birth to sin, whereas the Word of God has caused us to come to the birth into salvation and the kingdom of God.

Thought

This gift that God has given us is far greater than us. The divine life that stirs within us is the same life that with four words brought the whole of the universe into being.

---

[39] Jn.1:12,13

Prayer

Father God, with what have you filled me? It is your own life deeply embedded in me, and slowly unfurling itself to transform me into your likeness. Through your Word, I become a partaker of the divine nature.[40]

---

[40] See 2.Pet.1:4

DAY SEVENTEEN

The Best Behaviour

1:19-21 (ESV)

Know this, my beloved brothers: let every person be quick to hear, slow to speak, slow to anger; for the anger of man does not produce the righteousness of God. Therefore put away all filthiness and rampant wickedness and receive with meekness the implanted word, which is able to save your souls.

Whatever God gives us, and puts within us, must affect our behaviour. The seed he places within us is a good seed and a holy seed, and it carries his DNA. Therefore, if God is good, and gives good things, then it stands to reason that his goodness is being sown into us. We, of all the people on the face of the earth, should be exhibiting something of the goodness of God. We should be, in essence, good people.

James tells us to "be quick to hear, slow to speak, slow to anger…" Eugene Peterson is great here, putting it in the Message as:

Post this at all the intersections, dear friends: Lead with your ears, follow up with your tongue, and let anger straggle along in the rear.

This thoroughly practical piece of wisdom will want to touch and affect all our conversations with each other. It is actually reinforced biologically: God gave us two ears and only one mouth. How many of us have regretted speaking too quickly before we had thoroughly heard the other person, and have made too quick a judgment?

Hearing does not usually produce anger. Hearing often diffuses and turns away anger. Anger is usually produced by hot, un-thought-through and sharp words. The Proverbs are helpful here:

A soft answer turns away wrath, but a harsh word stirs up anger.[41]

There is one whose rash words are like sword thrusts, but the tongue of the wise brings healing.[42]

James goes on to say that anger does not produce the righteousness of God. Instead, hot, angry words reveal something else. The Preacher's Commentary says that "in short, our words and outbursts of anger reveal the true person within us"[43].

James goes on to say that in order to bring this about in our lives, there are some things (plural) that we need to reject and there is something (singular) that we need to embrace. The things we need to get rid of are spoken of in very strong terms: "all filthiness" and "rampant wickedness". The Weymouth translation of the book puts it like this:

Ridding yourselves, therefore, of all that is vile and of the evil influences which prevail around you...

In a nutshell, James wants us to see that all sin, however it manifests itself, fouls up our lives, and it needs dumping.

Some people have difficulties and problems with Joshua's severe cleansing of the land that God has promised to give Israel. God had told him to have absolutely nothing to do with the inhabitants or their practices, but instead he was to totally purge the land. The reason was simple: left alive, they would begin to be a paralyzing and negative effect on the people of God. In much the same way, sinful practices must not be allowed to domesticate themselves in our lives. The only thing that must dwell within us is the Word of God. In fact, Paul would write to the believers at Colossae, "Let the word of Christ dwell in you richly..." (Col.3:16) This Word we must embrace and receive into our hearts. It is this Word that must be allowed to have effect on us. Peterson puts it quite poetically as he writes in the Message, "In simple humility, let our gardener, God, landscape you with the word, making

---

41 Prov.15:1
42 Prov.12:18
43 *The Preacher's Commentary*, commenting on Jas.1:20, e-sword.net

a salvation-garden of your life." Out with the weeds of the enemy and in with the living, life-giving, cleansing and empowering seed of God!

Thought

A garden, left to itself, will naturally become inundated with weeds. We need to welcome the activity of the divine gardener as he sows his seed into us. We then need to work with him in cultivating these seeds into profound fruitfulness.

Prayer

Dear Lord, help me to grow a beautiful garden with you, one that pleases you, and proves to be a blessing and a resource to those around me.

DAY EIGHTEEN

Practitioners of the Word

1:22-25 (ESV)

But be doers of the word, and not hearers only, deceiving yourselves. For if anyone is a hearer of the word and not a doer, he is like a man who looks intently at his natural face in a mirror. For he looks at himself and goes away and at once forgets what he was like. But the one who looks into the perfect law, the law of liberty, and perseveres, being no hearer who forgets but a doer who acts, he will be blessed in his doing.

In the last passage that we looked at, James told us to "receive with meekness the implanted word". It will do us good to think about this, because how we receive the Word of God is vitally important. The word "meekness" (the NASB and the NIV translate the Greek word 'prautēs' as "humility") describes, not so much an outward manifestation of meekness, but an inward disposition. It's an attitude rather than an action. Kenneth Wuest would describe it as "that temper of spirit that accepts the dealings of God without disputing or resisting"[44]. I would add that it also means to receive the words of God in the same spirit. A good question to ask ourselves is, how does the Word of God find entrance into my heart – easily or with difficulty?

James then goes on to show the difference between 'the heard word' and 'the practised word'. We can see if the Word has really gained entrance because, if it has, it will be outworked in our everyday living. A word that has been incarnated will be evident, not only in our

---

[44] Kenneth S. Wuest, *Word Studies in the Greek New Testament,* Vol.3, Studies in the Vocabulary, (Eerdmans, Michigan, 1973), p.105

conversation, but also in our behaviour. James tells us not to be hearers only but doers – practitioners – of the word. Hearing without practising leads to self-deception; that is his clear message.

He then gives us an example. He says that it is like someone looking at his face in a mirror and then turning away, forgetting at once what he looks like. It will help us to remember the parable of the sower. There Jesus taught that the seed that fell on the unreceptive and hardened soil was immediately snatched away by the devil. But when the seed was received with an open and honest heart, there was growth and development. How we listen and how we receive are of vital importance. A word that is received with faith by the hearer, and meets with faith in the hearer, becomes activated within the hearer.

There are then three active words that James uses concerning the reading of the Scriptures. The first word is "look". The Greek word here is 'parakuptō', and it means 'to stoop to look at'. In other words, this is a deliberate and a prolonged looking, and there is the definite sense that we have to bend to it. The next word is "persevere". The Greek word here is 'paramenō', and it means 'to stay close'. That basically means that we stick with it, and we stick at it. There will be times when our Bible reading is difficult, and we feel nothing is happening. That is exactly the time when we need to push through our feelings and stay with it. Confucius once said that "the man who removed the mountain began by carrying away small stones"[45]. C.H. Spurgeon wrote, "By perseverance the snail reached the ark."[46] The third word is "act". We learn to forgive by forgiving; we learn to love by loving; we learn to pray by praying; we learn to give by giving. The Greek word is 'poiētēs', and means 'to perform'. It also means 'a poet', who creates something beautiful with words. This, then, is the beautiful practising of the word, creating a beautiful life.

There then follows a great promise to those who will pick up on these three action words. "He will be blessed in all his doing." As we take the Word of God into our hearts humbly and seriously, giving it our full attention, we will have the promise of blessing on all our activities. According to Psalm 1, the man who gives also himself to this

---

[45] Confucius, *Confucius: The Analects,* retrieved from
    http://www.goodreads.com/quotes/64564
[46] Charles Spurgeon, *Spurgeon's Gems,* retrieved from
    http://www.brainyquote.com

Word is blessed in everything that he does. Surely that is worth working towards!

Thought

My attitude toward the Word of God is crucial. To hear the voice of God in the Scriptures, I need to approach them quietly, slowly, reverently and with a child-like heart.

Prayer

Lord, open my eyes that I may behold wonderful things out of your law.[47]

---

47 See Psa.119:18

DAY NINETEEN

Pure Religion

1:26,27 (ESV)

If anyone thinks he is religious and does not bridle his tongue but deceives his heart, this person's religion is worthless. Religion that is pure and undefiled before God the Father is this: to visit orphans and widows in their affliction, and to keep oneself unstained from the world.

James now finishes off this section by seeking to apply what he has been teaching. In this particular passage, he contrasts two kinds of religion: one that is worthless and one that is pure. The word "religion" that is used here describes a kind of careful and ceremonious religious practice, where there is a meticulous effort in making sure that it is right and proper. The Greek word is 'thrēskeia', and it only used here. It means 'ceremonial service'. Edwin Hatch wrote:

> *It refers to the external observances of public worship, such as church attendance, almsgiving, prayer, fasting (Matt.6:1-18). It is the Pharisaic element in Christian worship.*[48]

The worthless religion, then, is where a person spends a lot of effort on the presentation and the keeping up the appearances in religious services, yet has no control whatsoever on his or her tongue. We will find that if we inadvertently tread on the corns of such an outwardly devout person, we will quickly see what James meant!

We have to remember, at this point, that words play a large part in our spirituality. Right from Genesis to Revelation there is huge

---

[48] Edwin Hatch, *Essays in Biblical Greek*, cited by Robertson's Word Pictures, commenting on Jas.1:26, e-sword.net

emphasis on words, and especially words that come from God. Words are a powerful medium, and can have tremendous effect. Those that understand this, receive them and use them wisely. Words express who we really are. Jesus taught that "out of the abundance of the heart the mouth speaks". (Matt.12:34) This is especially so when we are suddenly under pressure.

James teaches that the authentically spiritual person will learn to bridle his tongue. The word "bridle" is from the Greek word 'chalinagōgeō', and it means 'to hold in check or to restrain'. Here's a thought: we often want to bridle the tongues of others, but we are often reluctant to bridle our own. A well-known proverb reads, "When words are many, transgression is not lacking, but whoever restrains his lips is prudent." (Prov.10:19)

James then goes on to write about what authentic religion is really all about, and he says just two things:

> *Real religion, the kind that passes muster before God the Father, is this: Reach out to the homeless and loveless in their plight, and guard against corruption from the godless world.*[49]

In other words, if we take good care of the poor, and the powerless, and keep ourselves 'unstained' from the world, we will be manifesting an authentic faith. An authentic spirituality is neither self-centred nor egocentric. It is focused on the poor and the vulnerable. An authentic spirituality will walk very close to Jesus so that the passion of his heart touches and invades our own heart. Christ was anointed to preach good news to the poor, to reach out with healing and help to those who were broken-hearted and impoverished in spirit. A true contemplative will be enabled to see the face of God, and then to hear his heart, and also to hear the cries of others.

Therefore, we are called to go deeply into the world, and not to hide from it. We are called to act as 'salt and light' to the world, and yet not to be contaminated or corrupted by the world. The Greek word is 'aspilos', and means 'uncorrupted, unspotted, uncontaminated'. That's the effect this present world has on us. It stains us and it corrupts us. We nevertheless have to be in there, getting dirt on our hands and dirt on our feet, but never in our minds, our hearts, our conversations

---

[49] The Message

and our practices. We must never ever let the world dictate our thoughts, values and practices. We are called to present a viable, clean and authentic alternative. May God help us to do so.

Thought

Be very clean on the inside, and allow yourself to get dirty on the outside. Let it never be the other way around.

Prayer

Lord, deliver me from being too concerned about any outward shows of spirituality. Help me to be more concerned about my inner life – the developing of a pure-hearted compassion.

DAY TWENTY

Partiality

2:1-5 (NLT)

My dear brothers and sisters, how can you claim to have faith in our glorious Lord Jesus Christ if you favor some people over others? For example, suppose someone comes into your meeting dressed in fancy clothes and expensive jewelry, and another comes in who is poor and dressed in dirty clothes. If you give special attention and a good seat to the rich person, but you say to the poor one, "You can stand over there, or else sit on the floor" – well, doesn't this discrimination show that your judgments are guided by evil motives? Listen to me, dear brothers and sisters. Hasn't God chosen the poor in this world to be rich in faith? Aren't they the ones who will inherit the Kingdom he promised to those who love him?

I guess that this is one of the places where chapter and verse divisions aren't very helpful. James is still continuing his theme of being practitioners of the Word of God. Two benchmarks of genuine Christianity are, firstly, to pay special attention to the bereaved and afflicted, whilst keeping yourselves unstained from the world, (1:27) and secondly, to love your neighbour as yourself. (2:8) Coming up against and resisting these benchmarks was a prevailing attitude in the church that was very reminiscent of an old way of thinking. There was something in the Jewish, and especially the Pharisaic, psyche that quickly distanced itself from the unclean and those who did not share their particular brand of faith.

Commentators are agreed that the majority of those who attended church meetings in the first century were poor people. Paul would write to the church at Corinth, for example, saying, "Consider your calling, brothers: not many of you were wise according to worldly standards, not many were powerful, not many were of noble birth." (1.Cor.1:26) There doesn't seem to have been much of a middle class; people were either poor or they were rich. The poor were in the vast majority, and the rich and influential were in the tiny minority.

The poor man in our text is a very poor man. The word that is used to describe him is 'ptochos'. There is another word for 'poor' in the Greek language, 'autodiakonos', which simply means 'self-serving'. This other kind of 'poorness' is indicative of the man who says to himself, "I may not have fine clothes, or a fine house, or fine furnishings, but I can look after myself and my family. I don't need any charity, thank you." The first word, 'ptochos', however, describes a man who is absolutely destitute, having no means of visible support. This man is rendered powerless by his poverty; he is completely helpless. What do you think would be the equivalent of such a man today?

James picks up a big word to describe the attitude and behaviour of some of the church members in the assembly. The word is a compound word, 'prosōpolēpsia', and can be literally translated 'the accepting of a face'. To put this into a modern idiom, it is like saying to certain people, "Your face fits here," and to others, "Your face doesn't fit here." Other translations have it as "personal favouritism" (NASB), "snobbery" (J.B. Phillips), "making distinctions" (Weymouth).

James fires off a broadside here in saying this attitude is totally incompatible with genuine faith in Christ. Christ is the Lord of glory, and his face and his glory can be, should be, and are to be seen in the lowliest of his children. Mother Theresa was once asked how it was that she could so deeply and personally embrace the poor, especially those whom she found lying in the streets of Calcutta. She replied that she would gaze at them until she could see the face of Christ in them, and then she would minister to them as she would to Him. Whether she was meeting royalty, or those whom society had rejected, she would treat them exactly the same – she would love and serve them as if she was loving and serving Jesus Himself.

Thought

With the poor, the treasure is often found in their hearts, not on their clothes. And if we engage sincerely with them, we will certainly find it.

Prayer

Dear Lord, please take any trace of a despising attitude out of my heart, and help me to see and feel as you do towards the destitute around me.

DAY TWENTY-ONE

God's Values

The man lay in an alleyway, curled up in a cardboard box. Mother Theresa approached him, and fought through the overwhelming smell of an unwashed and vermin-ridden body. She took his hand, and he stirred and stared up at her. He then said, "It's years since I have felt the warmth of a human hand."

What empowered Mother Theresa to be able to do that? Very simply, it was the love of Christ. She had often told others who had asked that very same question, "I look intently into their faces until I can see the face of my Saviour, and then I love and serve them as I would him." The lesson is clear: if we cannot love the unlovely, then we cannot be in love with the Saviour.

One day, in conversation with his disciples, about the final Day, Jesus said:

> Then the King will say to those on his right, 'Come, you
> who are blessed by my Father, inherit the kingdom prepared
> for you from the foundation of the world. For I was hungry
> and you gave me food, I was thirsty and you gave me drink,
> I was a stranger and you welcomed me, I was naked and you
> clothed me, I was sick and you visited me, I was in prison
> and you came to me.' Then the righteous will answer him,
> saying, 'Lord, when did we see you hungry and feed you, or
> thirsty and give you drink? And when did we see you a
> stranger and welcome you, or naked and clothe you? And
> when did we see you sick or in prison and visit you?' And
> the King will answer them, 'Truly, I say to you, as you did
> it to one of the least of these my brothers, you did it to me.[50]

---

[50] Matt.25:34-40

We find here, I believe, an inviolable principle: the face of the Saviour can be, and needs to be, seen in the lowliest of his children. It seems, at least to Jesus, that the way we view them, value them, treat them, speak to them and act towards them reflects our true appreciation for Jesus himself. We can say a lot, we can pray a lot, we can even sing worship songs a lot, but our actions and attitudes give us away. When we are swayed and put off by the social standing of the poor and marginalised, we are out of touch with authentic Christianity.

How does God value the poor? How he values them is reflected in the way he treats them. Perhaps the classic text here is the one found in Phil.2:5-8:

> *Have this mind among yourselves, which is yours in Christ Jesus, who, though he was in the form of God, did not count equality with God a thing to be grasped, but emptied himself, by taking the form of a servant, being born in the likeness of men. And being found in human form, he humbled himself by becoming obedient to the point of death, even death on a cross.*

Another classic text would be the one found in 2.Cor.8:9:

> *For you know the grace of our Lord Jesus Christ, that though he was rich, yet for your sake he became poor, so that you by his poverty might become rich.'*

Christ did not look down on poverty; he embraced it for our sakes. From the first instance, he made his entrance into a filthy stable, and laid his head in a feeding trough. Somehow I get the feeling that the gospel is tilted somewhat towards those who are poor and powerless. Somebody has to speak and act for them, and a genuine experience of the love of God will want to take us in and among them.

Thought

My estimation and my feelings towards the poor and disadvantaged of this world is a pretty accurate reading of the true levels of my actual estimation and feelings towards Christ.

Prayer

Lord, please open my eyes to see what you see, and please open my heart to feel what you feel, and grant me the compassion, the grace and the courage to live accordingly.

DAY TWENTY-TWO

God's Choices

After stating that partiality, choosing 'whose face fits' in the assembly, is totally inconsistent with a genuine faith in Christ, James goes on to bolster his point with a fictitious example. He firstly introduces two men who came into the church. These two men were poles apart when it came to social standing in the community. Kenneth Wuest, in his Expanded Translation of the New Testament describes them in this way:

> *A man whose hand is conspicuously loaded with gold rings and in brightly shining clothing, and ... a poor man in dirty clothing who is dependent upon others for support.*[51]

What a contrast!

James then highlights two attitudes that were present in the church. One man, the rich man, is honoured and deferred to, and the other man, the poor man, is actually dishonoured and asked to distance himself. The thing that is betrayed here is an underlying attitude of respect for riches and social standing. The church members would never have said so, but their attitudes and actions gave them away.

In verse 5, James gives us a clear picture of God's values and God's choices. God has chosen the 'ptochoi' (the utterly destitute) of this world to be stunningly rich in faith. One commentator wrote that "poverty throws you into God; whilst riches lull you into a false sense of security". The poor have no options but to trust; whilst the rich have plenty of options. God has chosen the 'ptochoi' with the specific purpose of making them rich in faith. Peter, when faced with a lame pauper who reached out to him for some money at the Beautiful Gate,

---

[51] Kenneth S. Wuest, *The New Testament – an Expanded Translation*, (Eerdmans, Michigan, 1961), p.541

responded and said, "I have no silver and gold, but what I do have I give to you. In the name of Jesus Christ of Nazareth, rise up and walk!" (Acts 3:6)

I remember reading about the 13th Century theologian Thomas Aquinas having a conversation with the Renaissance Pope, Pope Innocent II. The Pope began to show Thomas the abundance of treasures that were to be seen in the chapel. "You see, Thomas," said the Pope, "the church can no longer say, 'Silver and gold have I none.'" "True," Thomas replied, "but neither can she now say, 'In the name of Jesus Christ, rise and walk.'"

James also goes on to write that these poor people are heirs of the kingdom. All the riches of heaven are at their disposal. This reminds me of the first beatitude: "Blessed are the poor ['ptochos'] in spirit. For theirs is the kingdom of heaven." (Matt.5:3) This is the stuff of the kingdom. We can either line our own pockets or we can empty them and invest in heaven. We can even do both, but the question is, where is our focus, our treasure?

The richness of heaven is given to those who love him. It's not given so much to those who make statements of faith, or those who give themselves in tireless service. It is given to those who love him. Sacrificial love is the language and the currency of heaven. And if we truly love him, then we will truly love those whom he loves, and they can often be the unlovely.

One commentator writes:

> *When you love another with Christ's love, you are always at eye level. You can neither look up at another nor down. Everyone who comes into our lives is on one level, whether rich or poor, bathed or unbathed, impressive or unimpressive.[52]*

God loves them all equally, and so must we. Indeed, the church should be the one social institution where all are treated equally. All are loved. The true love of Christ does not discriminate, and neither should we.

---

[52] *The Preacher's Commentary*, commenting on Jas.2:7, e-sword.net

Thought

The cross of Christ is the great leveller. For some it humbles us; for others it lifts us up.

Prayer

Father, your treasure is found in earthen vessels; in the frail and broken hearts of the lovers of your son. Help me to treasure what you treasure.

DAY TWENTY-THREE

Despising the Poor

2:6,7 (NLT)

But you dishonor the poor! Isn't it the rich who oppress you and drag you into court?

We stay with this a little longer because James stays with it in his letter. He is not making a little passing comment here on how the church treated the poor; rather he is making a strong point. He is challenging thought-patterns and deeply held attitudes. A.M. Hunter wrote of James that throughout all of his writing, there "glows a prophetic passion which stamps him as the Amos of the New Testament"[53].

He says that when we discriminate and become partial in our treatment of people, according to the cut of their clothes or whether their face fits or not, we are in fact dishonouring them. The Greek word used, 'atimazō', means 'to dishonour, to insult, to treat with contempt – whether in word, deed or thought'. In Jewish thought, whenever we snub the poor, we are in fact snubbing the 'Shekinah' glory of God and we are in grave danger of seeing it depart. James Adamson, in his commentary on James, describes "the sighing of the poor" as that which "banishes the Shechinah".[54] I once had a glance through the 170 references to the poor in the Bible, and the overall impression is that God is somewhat defensive over the way they are valued and treated.

---

[53] A.M. Hunter, *Introducing the New Testament*, (SCM Press Ltd, London, 1946), p.98

[54] James Adamson, *The Epistle of James*, (Eerdmans, Michigan, 1976), p.110

Dr R.W. Dale, in his commentary on James, says:

> *To do honour to a man simply because he is rich, no matter how he got his wealth or how he spends it; to forgive him all his vices, to exaggerate all his virtues, because he is rich – this is a crime. And if to this be added contempt for the poor, though their poverty may be dignified with uncomplaining patience, and faultless integrity, and unwearying industry – the crime becomes still more flagrant.*[55]

James goes on to talk about the rich. At first glance, one would think by now that he has some kind of grudge against them, but a little digging reveals otherwise. The Bible has nothing against being rich, but has a lot to say about how riches are handled. The rich in this case are using their power to oppress the poor, dragging them into court and blaspheming the name of Christ. The Greek word translated "oppress" is 'katadunasteuō'. It is a strong word, and it means 'to exercise harsh control over another, to use one's power against another'. It is used only in one other place, and that is in Acts 10:38, where it refers to those who are "oppressed" by the devil. The connection is stark. Money does talk, money can corrupt and money does exert power, sometimes oppressive power.

James Adamson, in his commentary writes:

> *To ill-treat the poor, therefore, was ipso facto to ill-treat Christ; for the Shekinah is said to suffer with those who suffer; he who strikes the cheek of an Israelite strikes, as it were, the cheek of the Shekinah.*[56]

The words and sighs of the poor are heard in heaven, and God honours those who honour the poor. A good question to ask ourselves is, what brings and keeps the Shekinah glory among us? Surely it is all in the realm of attitude. Maybe if we make an effort and seek to bring the poor and destitute near to our hearts, and welcome them among us, maybe, just maybe, the Shekinah glory of God will follow.

---

[55] R.W. Dale, *The Epistle of James and other Discourses*, (Hodder & Stoughton, London 1898), p.62

[56] James Adamson, *The Epistle of James*, the New International Commentary on the New Testament, (Eerdmans, Michigan, 1976), p.113

Thought

If we find within us desires to fill our churches with the right kind of people, that do not put others off from joining us, are we not building beautiful but empty shells?

Prayer

Lord, whom are you building your church with? Whom are you calling? Where are they coming from? Please align my prayers and my desires to your great heart.

DAY TWENTY-FOUR

The Royal Law

2:8-13 (NLT)

Yes indeed, it is good when you obey the royal law as found in the Scriptures: "Love your neighbor as yourself." But if you favor some people over others, you are committing a sin. You are guilty of breaking the law. For the person who keeps all of the laws except one is as guilty as a person who has broken all of God's laws. For the same God who said, "You must not commit adultery," also said, "You must not murder." So if you murder someone but do not commit adultery, you have still broken the law. So whatever you say or whatever you do, remember that you will be judged by the law that sets you free. There will be no mercy for those who have not shown mercy to others. But if you have been merciful, God will be merciful when he judges you.

How can you tell when a church is doing well? I guess we could all come up with some pretty good criteria. James has his own: a church that practises loving its neighbours as it loves itself is doing well. I would suggest that this refers to, not the practice of a few within the church, but the whole drift of the body of the church.

There are some interesting things to note out of this text. The law is called "the royal law". In other words, it is the law of a king. It has been called 'the royal law of love', and as such, this sums up the whole of the ethos of heaven. God is love, and everything he says is uttered out of a great heart of love. Every edict, every statute is born out of, and carries within it, overtones and undertones of love.

As we read these verses, our minds cannot help but go to a passage in the Gospel of Luke, where a certain lawyer asked Jesus for instructions concerning the inheriting of eternal life. Jesus responded to him by saying, "What is written in the law? How do you read it?" The lawyer came back with two commandments: "Love God passionately, and love your neighbour as you love yourself." Then came the loaded question from the lawyer: "Just who is my neighbour?" Jesus responded with the famous story of the Samaritan, who stopped to help someone who had been beaten up and robbed. The lawyer was shamed by the story. It exposed his deep-seated partiality and religious parochialism. A Samaritan was regarded as anathema by the Jewish community, and to think that he was fulfilling the royal law of love was almost unthinkable.

The key word in the Gospel passage, and also in the James' passage, is "mercy". God was not put off by the stench of our corruptness that had resulted out of our sinfulness. Instead, he came into the filthy arena, where we eked out our lives, and he ministered gently and tenderly to us, washing and healing our wounds, and he then spoke restorative words into our hearts. He filled us with hope when there was no hope. The incarnation was, in fact, mercy enacted. He came to where we were, because we were unable, and even unwilling, to get to where he was. The king who wrote the royal law came and practised it himself. The same mission is ours.

There is a church here in the city of Lincoln that has a 'leper's window' near the front door. It was built because the lepers were not allowed in the building. They could, however, take in it turn to peer longingly into the warmth of the building, as the saints sang their songs of worship, and the priest preached his sermons. The church was never designed to be a place of blessing to clean saints but refusing admittance to the unwashed and destitute. Many fear entering the doors of a church because they feel too ashamed, or they feel that they will be snubbed. We need to somehow turn that around. Mercy looks beyond the sinful reasons for their pitiable state, and learns to welcome, to embrace and to speak healing and restorative words. James says, "If you practise this one thing, you are doing well."

Thought

Francis of Assisi overcame his fear and embraced the leper, after hearing the Lord say to him, "What you used to abhor shall be to you joy and sweetness..."[57] At that point, he had mastered himself.

Prayer

Dear Lord, take the fear of the ugly and outwardly repulsive ones out of my heart, and replace it with such a compassion that will enable me to welcome and embrace them in your name.

---

[57] Johannes Jörgenson, *St Francis of Assisi*, translated by T. Connor Sloane (Image Books, New York, 1955), p.38,39

DAY TWENTY-FIVE

Mercy Triumphs Over Judgment

Some years ago, I attended a day conference, and was quite challenged when the speaker said at one point, "If the Bible is always affirming you and comforting you, and never making you feel uncomfortable, then you are probably misreading it." I believe that to be a true statement. The Scriptures must at times challenge what we believe and feel. The words of God not only heal and restore us, but they at times cut right into the core of our being, into the revealing of our hidden motives.

James comes back to this charge of partiality, not wanting to let us off the hook. He wants his readers to feel the seriousness of doing such a thing. If we practise partiality, he says, we are committing sin. More than that, to put it literally, we are 'working sin'. The rabbis taught that it was as serious as rebellion, and it was an affront, an insult, to the Shekinah glory of God.

In a Jewish tract entitled 'Shabbath', where there is dispute concerning the thirty-nine works commanded by Moses, Rabbi Yochanan says, "But if a man do the whole, with the omission of one, he is guilty of the whole, and of every one."[58] This is a rabbinical form of speech. James picks it up by basically saying, "We cannot pick and choose what commandments we want to obey. We cannot say that one is more important than another. God sees them as an integral whole." He writes, and I quote The Message here, "You can't pick and choose in these things specializing in keeping one or two things in God's law and ignoring others." The laws of heaven have to be seen as a whole – none more important than others – each integral to the others.

How then are we to think, speak and act? James talks about "speaking and acting as those who are to be judged under the law of

---

[58] Adam Clark, *Commentary on the Whole Bible,* e-sword.net

liberty". This is none other than the law of love, which, according to the Jamieson, Fausset and Brown commentary is "not a law of external constraint, but of internal, free, instinctive inclination"[59]. We have been set free from external regulations, and have been called to live according to a higher, more internal law – the law of love or the law of liberty. The commentary adds, "The law of liberty, through God's mercy, frees us from the curse of the law, that henceforth we should be free to love and obey willingly."[60] As we put ourselves under the liberating tutelage of the Spirit and the Word, we will find welling up within us new, stronger impulses of love and mercy. The new life that God has given us actually causes us to walk in his ways. (Ezek.36:27)

James finishes by saying that if we do not demonstrate mercy, then we will not find it ourselves. Here is a truth: heaven seems to treat us in the same way we treat others, and the significant others seem to be the least. Mercy triumphs over judgment. Chrysostom wrote:

> Mercy is clothed with the divine glory, and stands by the throne of God. When we are in danger of being condemned, she rises up and pleads for us, and covers us with her defence, and enfolds us with her wings.[61]

Mercy doesn't condemn; rather, it seeks to understand. Not only that, it seeks to heal and restore.

Thought

"Where mercy, love, and pity dwell, there God is dwelling too."[62] Is he dwelling with you?

Prayer

Dear God, please fill up my heart with mercy, and help me reflect well your great heart for this world.

---

[59] *Jamieson, Fausset and Brown commentary,* e-sword.net
[60] Ibid
[61] John Chrysostom, cited by Charles Ellicott, *Commentary on the Bible,* Vol.8 (Wipf and Stock Publishers, Oregon, 2015), p.365
[62] William Blake, *The Divine Image,* retrieved from http://www.poetryfoundation.org/poem/172912

DAY TWENTY-SIX

Faith without Works

2:14-17 (NLT)

What good is it, dear brothers and sisters, if you say you have faith but don't show it by your actions? Can that kind of faith save anyone? Suppose you see a brother or sister who has no food or clothing, and you say, "Good-bye and have a good day; stay warm and eat well" – but then you don't give that person any food or clothing. What good does that do? So you see, faith by itself isn't enough. Unless it produces good deeds, it is dead and useless.

Martin Luther, the great German reformer, did not like this epistle that James had written. He called it "an epistle of straw", stating as his reasons that in his view, there was nothing evangelical in it, and that it had no apostolic authority about it.[63] He felt that the letter gave far too much attention to works. Coming out from the dominating spiritual influence of medieval Catholicism, it is plain to see that his remarks were an unfortunate overreaction.

Paul, in his great letter to the Ephesians, teaches us that we are not saved *by* good works, but that we are saved *for* good works. There is nothing that we can do to get us into heaven, but heaven has plenty for us to do, and it has all been prepared for us to discover and step into. Paul wrote:

---

[63] William Barclay, *The Letters of James and Peter*, The Daily Study Bible, (St Andrew Press, Edinburgh, 1993), pp.6,7

For we are his workmanship, created in Christ Jesus for good works, which God prepared beforehand, that we should walk in them.[64]

James tells us that faith by itself will not save us. If our beliefs produce nothing except creedal statements and hymns and choruses, then we have missed something. God didn't sing and speak about salvation; God actually stepped down and into our world and enacted salvation, and therein is our model. The biblical history is full of the activity of God. Faith is the root of our salvation and works are the fruit of our salvation. One naturally will produce the other, and if works are not apparent, then one must question the genuineness of the faith.

The Jerusalem church had been in the throes of a severe famine. A travelling prophet called Agabus had foreseen it, and many of the churches that Paul had founded had sent money to alleviate their hardships. Many in the church would have suffered deprivation, and what James is saying here is set into the context of how we think of, speak to and treat the poor among us. In the case of the brother who is poorly clothed (the word used is 'gumnos' – 'naked; not enough to cover him') and lacking in food, words of blessing alone will not help him. Pious words of love and blessing from within the safe boundaries of church life will save no-one. The apostle John wrote:

If anyone has the world's goods and sees his brother in need, yet closes his heart against him, how does God's love abide in him? Little children, let us not love in word or talk but in deed and in truth.[65]

The rabbis taught that "if a man gives only one coin to a poor brother, he becomes worthy to receive the face of the Shekinah"[66].

James said that faith without works is dead. Three times in the epistle he repeats this.[67] A professed and sung faith without the love of God that reaches out to others in action is an empty husk, a parody of Christianity, and like the fig tree that promised the fruit of figs but

---

[64] Eph.2:10

[65] 1.Jn.3:17,18

[66] Yalqut on Psa.17; b. *Baba Bathra* 10a, cited by James Adamson, *The Epistle of James*, the New International Commentary on the New Testament, (Eerdmans, Michigan, 1976), p.122

[67] 2:17,20,26

revealed only leaves, it will wither under the gaze of Christ. A genuine love of God is authenticated by a practical love for the needy ones around us – a love that goes far beyond well-meaning words into well-thought-through actions.

Thought

God has planned this day already for you to walk into. He has things for you to do.

Prayer

Dear God, this morning I woke up into a day that you had already been at work on. Show me my part to play in your kingdom today.

DAY TWENTY-SEVEN

Faith Alone?

2:18-26 (NLT)

Now someone may argue, "Some people have faith; others have good deeds." But I say, "How can you show me your faith if you don't have good deeds? I will show you my faith by my good deeds." You say you have faith, for you believe that there is one God. Good for you! Even the demons believe this, and they tremble in terror. How foolish! Can't you see that faith without good deeds is useless? Don't you remember that our ancestor Abraham was shown to be right with God by his actions when he offered his son Isaac on the altar? You see, his faith and his actions worked together. His actions made his faith complete. And so it happened just as the Scriptures say: "Abraham believed God, and God counted him as righteous because of his faith." He was even called the friend of God. So you see, we are shown to be right with God by what we do, not by faith alone. Rahab the prostitute is another example. She was shown to be right with God by her actions when she hid those messengers and sent them safely away by a different road. Just as the body is dead without breath, so also faith is dead without good works.

In the previous verses, we looked at the attitude of what Alec Motyer has called the "armchair philanthropist"[68]. This is the description of the man who sees the needs of the poor, mutters

---

[68] J. A. Motyer, *The Message of James: The Tests of Faith*, (IVP, London, 1970), p.55

84

some words of pious comfort, and then moves on without lifting a finger to help. He sees the man's predicament, but he does not engage with it. James is blistering about such expressions of faith. He basically says that faith without works is like a corpse. It is a corpse and not a man, having the form but not the life.

He then moves on to bring a comparison between a real faith and an empty faith. But first we need some background to put all this in context. The apostle Paul had taught that God wanted faith – expressed in the finished work of Christ. The Jewish nation, however, had been taught that God wanted action; in other words, practise the law and you will invoke the favour of God. There were two camps within the church. Was it a life of faith or was it a life of action? James was saying that it is both, but in the right order. Works come out of faith.

Real faith is active. Paul Mizzi, in his essay on 'Faith and Works', wrote that faith "is a personal act, involving the mind, the heart and will". He also taught that "faith involves three steps or aspects: knowledge, agreement and trust".[69] We learn the truth, we agree with the truth, and then we step out in the truth. To say that all I need is faith is like the man who says, "I have money." It's one thing to have it, but what are you going to do with it?

Real works are actions that flow out of faith. Paul talks about the "work of faith".[70] A genuine faith in Christ will inspire action. Alec Motyer called the life of faith "the life of consecrated action, of practised obedience to whatever God may command"[71]. Our faith is visible to God and invisible to men, but it is nevertheless revealed to men by our deeds of obedience. Real faith can be shown and demonstrated. If there is no fruit, then there is something wrong with the root. Jesus told a parable about a man who found himself at the wedding feast without a wedding garment. The apostle John also tells us that the fine linen of the saints is their righteous deeds.[72] So, the man's testimony got him in there, but his lack of clothing got him thrown out! That's an interesting theology!

Real faith is not merely mental assent to the truth of God. According to Mark's Gospel, the first one to recognize Jesus as the Son

---

[69] Paul Mizzi, *Essay on Faith and Works*, http://www.tecmalta.org/tft.htm

[70] 1.Thess.1:3/2.Thess.1:11

[71] J. A. Motyer, *The Message of James: The Tests of Faith*, (IVP, London, 1970), p.54

[72] Rev.19:8

of God was a demon. (Mk.1:24) The demons have no problem in believing who Jesus is, but their only reaction to that truth is to tremble. Motyer wrote that if the first example of spurious faith was the "armchair philanthropist", then the second is that of "believing demons".[73] The Greek word James uses for "tremble" is 'phrissō', and it means 'to bristle'. In other words, they stiffen up, and their hair stands up in horror with unspeakable and paralyzing fear. Their knowledge is not faith; rather it is a paralysing knowledge of their fate. Real faith, on the other hand, is not paralysed, but acts on what we know and believe. James also writes that faith apart from works is "useless". The Greek word used here is 'nekros' – literally 'a corpse'! Since a real faith will unite us to Christ, it cannot then be lifeless, but it must grow, and express itself visibly and powerfully to those around us.

Thought

> Use your heads! Do you suppose for a minute that you can cut faith and works in two and not end up with a corpse on your hands?[74]

Faith must express itself in order to breathe.

Prayer

Dear Lord, as I inhale faith into my heart today, help me to exhale it in some act of kindness.

---

[73] Ibid, p.55
[74] Jas.2:20 (The Message)

DAY TWENTY-EIGHT

The Example of Abraham

In the footnotes of the ESV Reformation Bible, the comment on Jas.2:22 reads, "The full outworking of faith is seen in works. True faith always produces fruit. Faith and works may be distinguished, but never separated or divorced."[75] Eugene Peterson, in the Message, calls faith and works "yoked partners".

James now goes on to give the first of two examples of expressed faith. Out of all the biblical characters available, he picks Abraham the friend of God and Rahab the prostitute. Alec Motyer, in his little commentary on James, wonders that the Word of God brings these two together as examples of faith: a man and a woman, a Jew and a Gentile, a saint and a harlot.[76]

Both Paul and James hold Abraham up as an example of faith. Paul, however, refers to Gen.15, where Abraham is told to look at the heavens and count the stars. The word of the Lord then comes saying, "So shall your offspring be."[77] Abraham believes the Lord, and it is counted to him as righteousness. He is justified before God by simply believing what God has said to him. James, on the other hand, refers to Gen.22, where God tells Abraham to sacrifice his son Isaac. Now why would God do that?

The first reason is that faith has to be tested. The scripture tells us that in this matter, God was testing Abraham. Everything God does in us has to be tested to see whether it has been genuinely received, and whether it has taken root in us. It is one thing to profess belief; it is

---

[75] *The Reformation Study Bible,* comment on Jas.2:22, (Ligonier Ministries, Sanford, 2005), p.1803

[76] J. A. Motyer, *The Message of James: The Tests of Faith*, (IVP, London, 1970), p.58

[77] Gen.15:5

entirely another thing to act on that belief. I was once speaking to a prisoner in a high security prison who had professed a faith in God. I said to him, "It's good that you believe in him; now you have to trust him."

Alec Motyer writes:

> *Faith must be challenged; if, in the face of the challenge, it is victorious, then it makes progress towards becoming a fixed characteristic of life, and moves on to genuine maturity. Abraham came to maturity when the faith he expressed in Gen.15:6 proved victorious in the face of the challenge of Gen.22:1f.*[78]

Genuine faith matures in the fire of testing.

The second reason was – and these are my own feelings speaking here – that Abraham loved Isaac just that little bit too much. For years his faith had been in God, and now that the promise had been fulfilled, his faith resided in his son. Now the visible was present, the need for the invisible had receded. It was as if God was saying, "He is too deeply in your heart, Abraham. I will brook no rivals. Sacrifice him." After a night of agonizing inner wrestling, Abraham obeyed God. He trusted God's word that he would be the father of nations, despite what was before him now. The writer to the Hebrews tells us that he actually got to a place where he believed that God would raise Isaac from the dead. This is faith tested to the limits. This is faith demonstrating that God comes first in all things. This is faith matured and faith purified. And that's a good thing, isn't it?

Thought

When the fruit of our faith becomes the focus of our faith, then it will turn bad on us. Don't let the vision become an idol. Keep your eyes on the Lord.

Prayer

Jesus, keep me focused on the unseen, and do not let my heart be swayed by the visible, however fruitful it may be.

---

[78] Ibid, p.56

DAY TWENTY-NINE

The Example of Rahab

The whole theme of this little section of the letter of James is that genuine faith is irrevocably allied to works. They are different, and they are inseparable, and they flow together in sequence. We do not come to faith through works; we do works because of our faith.

We now come to the second example of expressed faith, namely that of Rahab the harlot. There are similarities, in that she acted on her faith, but that is all. Rahab was a woman, a pagan and a prostitute. Just this fact alone inspires us. You don't have to be a great saint to express genuine faith. Rahab's faith was infantile, and there is no evidence that she had desisted from her rather disreputable lifestyle. James does not give approval to that lifestyle; rather, he points to the acts of faith that came out of her limited revelation of God.

We find her story in the second chapter of the book of Joshua. It is interesting that the two spies sent by Joshua should choose to lodge in her house. It was probably the only place where they could hope to remain undetected, and it was on the wall, giving opportunity for a quick escape if needed. It certainly had the directive hand and blessing of God all over it. However, it was noticed and it was reported to the king, and Rahab, instead of doing her patriotic duty, hid the two men and lied to the deputation that had been sent to arrest them.

In the house, the two men quickly discovered that the woman had a pretty good understanding of how events really were unfolding. She acknowledged that it was felt by the people that the Lord had given the land to Israel. It seemed that everyone was in fear and trembling because they had heard of the parting of the Red Sea, and the destruction of the two great kings of the Amorites. The news had 'melted the hearts' of everyone. Rahab then made this statement, and here we see her faith: "...for the LORD your God, he is God in the heavens above and on the earth beneath." (Josh.2:11b) Upon that simple knowledge, she took the decision to take her own life in her hands to save the lives of the two men of Israel.

Not only did she save the two spies, but she and her family were saved. The house where they were living was on the wall, and I guess that part of the wall did not fall down. She and those she loved were spared, and she went on to marry an Israeli by the name of Salmon. A more remarkable fact is that she and her husband are mentioned in the genealogy of Jesus in the first chapter of Matthew's Gospel. It's always amazing to see whom God will use to further his purpose: believing patriarchs and believing prostitutes.

The passage finishes off by reasserting the lesson that faith apart from works is dead. Faith is the root of our spiritual life and works are the fruit. We should not have one without the other. Faith without works is like a body without the breath of life in it. It is merely a corpse. Let us then ensure that our faith is a living faith, manifesting itself in vibrant works of goodness, reflecting the heart of the Father.

Thought

The grace and mercy of God is always larger than our concepts of both. He sees far more than we do.

Prayer

Dear Lord, I may not be either an Abraham or a Rahab, but I believe that even I can act on your words. Show me how to do so today.

DAY THIRTY

The Responsibility of Teachers

3:1,2 (ESV)

Not many of you should become teachers, my brothers, for you know that we who teach will be judged with greater strictness. For we all stumble in many ways. And if anyone does not stumble in what he says, he is a perfect man, able also to bridle his whole body.

James now turns his attention to a subject that he touched on earlier in his letter: the use of the tongue. In 1:26, he told the readers to "be slow to speak", and in 1:26, he wrote, "If anyone thinks he is religious and does not bridle his tongue but deceives his heart, this person's religion is useless."

In this particular passage, James issues a strong warning against would-be teachers. We have to remember here that he was speaking into a predominantly Jewish church. It was the dream of any Jewish parent that their son would become a rabbi because the role carried with it status, power and privileges. Coupled with the early church practice of 'body ministry', the temptation to become noticed, well thought of and well known was very powerful.

The gift-ministry of 'teacher' in the early church was up there with 'apostles' and 'prophets'. In Acts 13, the church was governed by prophets and teachers. This was a different level of teaching ability and anointing from that of local elders who had to be "able to teach"[79]. The Eph.4:11 gift-ministries were trans-local.

James wanted to point out that with the job there came a responsibility, and with the responsibility there came accountability. In

---

[79] 1.Tim.3:2

my view, leadership in any shape or form is more about taking weight-bearing responsibility than great gifts and exerting power over people.

R.W. Dale, in a little commentary on James published in 1898, spoke of a young Christian who was asked to speak on a difficult biblical issue. Dale made the comment:

> [Some] imagine that what they can read in an hour ought to be enough to enable them to form a final judgment on the greatest questions which perplex human thought.[80]

Their knowledge would be rooted in a book that took an hour to read. They had then become authorities on the subject. The man who first mentored me in the Scriptures, the late Ralph Shallis, told me that over the years, many young men had come to him propounding their pet doctrines and theories. He said, "I will not even listen to them until they have read their bibles from cover to cover at least thirteen times." This seemingly harsh comment floored me, but upon later reflection, and in my later years, I began to fully realise the wisdom of his words. This showed me how we are too quick to speak on things. We would be better spending time listening, pondering, weighing up before we open our mouths.

The main tool of a teacher is the spoken word. Like any workman, mistakes can be made and some are quickly rectified. For a teacher, however, words spoken are difficult to retrieve. As one has put it, "It is like trying to squeeze the toothpaste back into the tube." Words are powerful. They shape and they colour our lives – for the better and also for the worse. James is saying that a teacher plays with fire. Fire can warm the soul, or fire can scorch and damage the soul. Jesus actually said that we would be "held accountable" for every careless word we uttered. (Matt.12:36) What is a careless word? Simply, it is a word that is spoken without thought, and without care for the person on the receiving end. Therefore, the heartbeat of a teacher should be that of a profound love for people.

Thought

We need to teach in order to shape and construct souls, not to distort and tear them apart. Be careful how you use your words today.

---

[80] R.W. Dale, *The Epistle of James and other Discourses*, (Hodder & Stoughton, London, 1898), p.88

Prayer

Dear Father, your first words were revealing, creative and restorative. They still are. Help me to catch your heart in this.

DAY THIRTY-ONE

It's Easy to Stumble

In the book of Ecclesiastes, there is a little verse that says, "The words of the wise are like goads, and like nails firmly fixed are the collected sayings; they are given by one Shepherd." (12:11) Goads and nails come from good teaching. The word "goad" speaks of a sharp-pointed stick that provokes and excites movement. A nail firmly fixed speaks of that which can support something that is hung upon it. The teachings of a good teacher are like inner prompts that remain and are so well established that you can lean on them. I have met and heard some teachers whose sermons have been seminal into my life. In other words, they have brought things to birth in me; they have sparked ideas into life, and they have created visions, concepts and dreams in me. They have laid the foundational footings upon which I have been able to build.

But James warns us that it is easy to stumble. Nobody is above contradiction. Unfortunately, there are those who think they are, who are convinced that how they see things is the only way to see them. Of all consciences, theirs is the most enlightened. Of all perceptions and viewpoints, theirs is the only correct one. This is nothing more than arrogance of the highest order. The hallmark of a good teacher is that he is always learning, totally convinced that the more he knows, the more he knows that he doesn't know; and that he is just as able to stumble as the next man.

James goes on to infer that if we are able to bridle the tongue then we are able to bridle the whole of our body. 'To bridle' means 'to bring under control, to restrain'. There are a number of thoughts that come out of this.

Firstly, words can easily slip out of our mouth. In the height of excitement – even when anointed! – or under a moment of extreme

94

pressure, or when alcohol has been flowing too freely, words can be spoken that are regretted later. Alcohol is often used to 'loosen the tongue'. There is a strong little proverb that says, "When words are many, transgression is not lacking..." (Prov.10:19)

Secondly, this highlights the need for us to live disciplined lives. Self-control is part of the fruit that the Holy Spirit wants to manifest in us. The other half of that proverb, you see, reads, "...but whoever restrains his lips is prudent." Solomon also wrote, "Whoever restrains his words has knowledge..." (Prov.17:27) The word translated "restrain" is the Hebrew word 'châsak', and it means 'to withhold, restrain, hold back, keep in check, refrain.' Think wild horses.

We should seek to exercise self-control in our speech, because according to James, our words can affect the whole of life. Our words, therefore, should match our lifestyle. There are to be found horrid exceptions to this, where the most powerful and eloquent of teachers have unsubdued areas of darkness within and around them. The effects, when that becomes apparent, are very damaging to the wider church. It is for this reason that teachers will be judged with greater strictness. As we acknowledge our proneness to mistakes, then, let us pray even more fervently the prayer of David found in Psa.141:3:

> Set a guard, O LORD, over my mouth; keep watch over the door of my lips!

Thought

Knowing also how precious people are to God, and knowing how powerful our words can be, we ought to become both thoughtful and skilful in our use of them.

Prayer

Dear Holy Spirit, dear Holy Dove of God, touch my lips today with your gentle anointing so that I may impart something from heaven into those I rub shoulders with.

DAY THIRTY-TWO

Bits and Rudders

3:3,4 (NLT)

*We can make a large horse go wherever we want by means
of a small bit in its mouth. And a small rudder makes a huge
ship turn wherever the pilot chooses to go, even though the
winds are strong.*

We are going to stay with this whole subject of the tongue for some time. James is devoting several verses to it, and the reason for that is, so much of our ministry is word-based. What we say, whether inadvertently or purposefully, can go a very long way.

Here, at this point, he introduces two very common illustrations. The first is that of a bit that is placed in the mouth of a horse, and the other is that of a rudder placed at the stern of a ship. There are a number of key thoughts that come out of these illustrations.

The first is that both the bit and the rudder are very small compared to where they are found. James wants to emphasise this. Whenever we look back to the cause of an argument, it was usually a very small matter that set it all off. It fact, it was usually just a small word, either taken out of context, or spoken out of frustration or anger.

The second thought is that small things guide great things. James is going to take this up in greater detail later. A powerful horse is guided by a small bit and a large ship is guided by a small rudder. The key word here is 'guide'. It is the Greek compound word 'metagōmen', and it is only used by James here. The word means 'transfer, to lead over, to turn around, to change the direction'. This is an important word, because James is saying that although the horse can move by itself wherever it wants to, and although the great ship can move at the mercy of the winds and waves, the power to control and guide is 'transferred' to the small bit and the small rudder, and instead of running loose, both horse and ship are turned around and brought under the control of another. The Greek of this can literally read, 'We make the horses change their direction,' and, 'The ships are made to change their course.'[81]

Let's apply this a little. Firstly, the words that I speak can control and influence my future, and also the future of others, either for the worse or for the better. The words that I choose to speak can bring my past and my present back into line with the plans and purposes of God for my life, and in ministry they can do the same for others as well. This little muscle in my mouth can turn my world around, and it can also turn the worlds of others around. It is for this reason that James places so much responsibility upon those who teach the Word.

Secondly, recognizing the power of this small muscle within us, it behoves us to seek to bring it under control. Amy Carmichael was a missionary in India and wrote a number of books – the smallest and most challenging being entitled 'If'. In it, she wrote, "If a sudden jar can cause me to speak an impatient, unloving word, then I know nothing of Calvary love."[82] She added a footnote: "For a cup brimful of sweet water cannot spill even one drop of bitter water however suddenly jolted." Jesus said, "Out of the abundance of the heart, the mouth speaks." (Matt.12:24) A good question to ask ourselves is this: what are we, in the depths of our being, full of? It will come out in our words, especially when we are jolted.

Thought

In the darkest and most traumatic moment of his life, the Lord Jesus spoke the Scriptures into a prayer. Now there's a goal to aim for.

Prayer

Dear Lord, when you were crushed, out of your mouth came words of broken sweetness. Help me to become more like you.

---

[81] James Adamson, *The Epistle of James*, the New International Commentary on the New Testament, (Eerdmans, Michigan, 1976), p.142
[82] *If;* Amy Carmichael

DAY THIRTY-THREE

Boasting of Great Things

3:5 (ESV)

So also the tongue is a small member, yet it boasts of great things. How great a forest is set ablaze by such a small fire!.

James continues his thought by stating how the tongue is a small member in the context of our whole body, yet it boasts of great things. See again the comparison between the words "small" and "great". This little muscle, living inside our mouth, yields such power and influence that it can get a bit too big for its boots! Asaph, a skilled musician, wrote Psalm 73, and in it he talks of the wicked:

> *They scoff and speak with malice; loftily they threaten oppression. They set their mouths against the heavens, and their tongue struts through the earth.[83]*

Many a tongue boasts, and when all is examined, it is nothing but a lot of wind. Listen to the wisdom of Solomon:

> *Be not rash with your mouth, nor let your heart be hasty to utter a word before God, for God is in heaven and you are on earth. Therefore let your words be few. For a dream comes with much business, and a fool's voice with many words ... For when dreams increase and words grow many, there is vanity.[84]*

This phrase "great things" is the Greek compound word 'megalaucheō', and it is found only here in the New Testament. It

---

[83]   verse 8
[84]   Eccles.5:2,3,7

means 'to vaunt, to be grandiloquent or speaking in a pompous manner'. All great speakers have learned to appreciate the power of the tongue. Whole crowds and even nations have been swayed by the powerful oratory of a man who knew the power of the spoken word. A king who rallies his anxious troops, a statesman who addresses the nation, an Adolf Hitler who could mesmerise his people into a dark war that became worldwide, a Winston Churchill who could stimulate the British people into never thinking of defeat. In good hands the tongue can inspire and empower; in the wrong hands the tongue can wreak havoc and pain. The NIV Commentary says, "The tongue is able to sway multitudes. It can alter the destinies of nations."[85]

Many years ago, an artless word was spoken off the cuff to me. Over the years, it sank itself into my subconscious, and then began to speak into my heart and mind. It began to shape and influence my thinking, my feelings and my planning. As time went on, I became aware of the crippling effect it was exerting on me. It had become a curse. After prayer with a good friend, its power was broken and it was dismissed. God then spoke another word into my heart, and I have been living in the freedom of it ever since.

Imagine someone's tongue that has been brought under control by the power of the Holy Spirit, and imagine that same tongue being used to speak the words of God under the anointing of the Holy Spirit. Such speaking will carry enormous weight and influence. There is an old hymn that contains the words, "Take my tongue and let it be filled with messages for thee."[86]

Our tongue, when brought into subjection, and touched by the Spirit of God, can be the means of many people being fed, nourished, envisioned and quickened. This little muscle can move mountains and shape the personal worlds of those around us.

Thought

Speak to your brothers and sisters in Christ as you would speak to Jesus himself, and you won't go far wrong.

---

[85] *The New International Commentary, Vol.2,* commenting on Jas.3:5, (Hodder & Stoughton, London, 1994), p.1029

[86] Frances Ridley Havergal, *Take My Life,* No 519, Songs of Fellowship, Vol.1, (Kingsway Music, Eastbourne, 2003)

Prayer

Jesus, help me to see your face in the ones that I will speak to today in your name, and may I bless them as I would bless you.

DAY THIRTY-FOUR

The Tongue of Fire

3:6 (NLT)

And among all the parts of the body, the tongue is a flame of fire. It is a whole world of wickedness, corrupting your entire body. It can set your whole life on fire, for it is set on fire by hell itself.

I guess many of us have seen the devastating effects of a forest fire on the television screen at some point. Often hundreds of square miles of mature trees are destroyed, not to mention the loss of animal and plant life. On occasions, homes and people suffer as a result. Very often, at the root of it is a careless fire. Sometimes, it is done deliberately, but it doesn't take a lot to get it burning. And with the help of the wind, it is soon out of control, wreaking terrible havoc and carnage. In the same way, James says, we cannot imagine what we set loose when we open our mouths.

There is an interesting flow of thought here at this point. James tells us that the tongue is a fire. It has the effect of setting other things on fire, and it is set on fire itself by hell. James Adamson, in his commentary, gives the idea that the tongue is like "a fire (for example, an unguarded campfire) in a forest."[87] The imagery is strong.

James is right to tell us that the tongue is a fire. It ignites, it inflames. It can also bring warmth; or it can scorch and do damage. I find it interesting, and maybe a little ironic, that the Holy Spirit gave "tongues ... of fire"[88] on the day of Pentecost. Were they connected? Were they

---

[87] James Adamson, *The Epistle of James*, the New International Commentary on the New Testament, (Eerdmans, Michigan, 1976), p.144
[88] Acts 2:3

to both purify and empower? That would be the ideal, but sadly, it is not often the practice.

James wrote that it is also "a world of unrighteousness". In the Greek, it is "the unrighteous world" that is set into our body. In essence, it is a little evil, unjust world in miniature. This, according to Alec Motyer, is its character. He writes:

> *The world is everything that refuses to recognize the lordship of Christ, and that world, that unruliness, that opposition to God, has its standing representative, its permanent man among our faculties.*[89]

It is, if you like, a foreign embassy in our little kingdom. We are wise if we recognize it. Robertson's word picture makes this comment:

> *Clearly James means to say that the tongue can play havoc...*[90]

The tongue also has influence. James says that it actually stains or soils the whole body. Left to its own devices, its influence is almost always negative. That's why there is so much emphasis from the Bible to bring it under control. Words are of a neutral colour, but depending on what is behind them, they do exit our mouths coloured; they colour us, they colour atmospheres, they colour the worlds of those around us.

Then, we have its continuance. The tongue sets on fire the cycle of nature or the course of life. It touches the whole of our life from our early childhood to our old age. It never loses its potency. From the undisciplined and uninformed words of youth to the crabbiness and bitterness of the aged, it influences and touches everything.

Finally, the tongue has an affiliation. There is something behind it. James says that it is set on fire by hell. Just as the Holy Spirit's fire came down to mobilize the tongue for God, so there is a spirit from hell that can touch the tongue to bring about incredible destruction and deviation from God's paths. Even Peter, anxious for the welfare of his Master, could speak from a source that Jesus recognized as satanic.[91] This is strong stuff from James, but it does reinforce the care that we

---

[89] J. A. Motyer, *The Message of James: The Tests of Faith*, (IVP, London, 1970), p.65

[90] *Robertson's Word Pictures*, commenting on Jas.3:6, e-sword.net

[91] See Matt.16:23

need to take when we are opening our mouth and speaking. Let us be careful then with our words; let us discipline ourselves to use them to bless, encourage and may they be restorative in influence to broken lives living in this broken world in which we live.

Thought

> *The tongue can bring death or life; those who love to talk will reap the consequences.*[92]

What consequences would you like to see today out there in your world? You choose.

Prayer

Dear Lord, set a guard, over my mouth; keep watch over the door of my lips![93]

---

[92] Prov.18:21 (NLT)
[93] See Psa.141:3

DAY THIRTY-FIVE

The Restless Evil

3:7-8 (ESV)

For every kind of beast and bird, of reptile and sea creature, can be tamed and has been tamed by mankind, but no human being can tame the tongue. It is a restless evil, full of deadly poison.

By now, you may well be thinking, shall I open my mouth today? This little member in our mouth is of such importance that much has been written about it in Scripture. No other New Testament writer gives so much space and comment about the use of the human tongue than James does. The only other writer to match this is Solomon in his book of pithy proverbs. A careful muse through that book on the use of the tongue will reveal much.

So why does James use such strong language? Why is there such a strong emphasis on the tongue? In my view, James is saying that we must never, ever underestimate the power of this little muscle in our mouth. Solomon wrote, "Death and life are in the power of the tongue." (Prov.18:21) Wars have been unleashed and the dead have been raised by the use of the tongue.

James goes on to tell us that the tongue is untameable. The Greek word for "tame" is 'damazō', and literally means 'to tame, to curb, to restrain', and therefore we have an idea of something like a wild animal that cannot be restrained or controlled. James also tells us that the tongue is "a restless evil" (ESV/NASB) Other translations put it like this: "the tongue runs wild" (The Message), "it is an uncontrollable evil" (NLT), "an ever-busy mischief" (Weymouth), "an evil always likely to break out" (J.B. Phillips). The Greek word for "restless" is 'akataschetos', which means 'that which cannot be restrained'. The word literally means 'unrestrainable'. Left to its own devices, it is like a killer on the loose.

In Hebrew thought there is a very easy connection between the man and the members of his body. They are inseparable, and the man shares the guilt. Regarding a man and his hand, we often hear the words, "My hand slipped..." Regarding the tongue, we hear the excuse, "I couldn't help it; it just slipped out." Imagine, if you will, the scene where a pit bull terrier savages a child to death. Where does the fault lie? James is teaching us that you and I have a pit bull terrier in our mouth!

James goes on to say that the tongue is "full of deadly poison". The phrase literally means 'death-bearing poison'. Is it possible that such a little muscle can bring death? It can certainly create suspicion and thereby tarnish and destroy a reputation. It can certainly soil and stain a holy atmosphere and destroy a sense of the presence of the Lord. R.W. Dale, in his commentary on James, said:

> There may be poison – deadly poison – in words. They may destroy purity; they may destroy faith in God; they may destroy trust in men; they may destroy the mutual affection of friends; they may destroy the peace of families; they may destroy the very life of churches.[94]

James is very concerned that we come to terms with the seriousness of this matter. He is anxious that we fully understand the destructive power of this little member that lies between our teeth. Can it be tamed? Our hope is in the power of the Holy Spirit. But even Spirit-filled men and women are not guiltless of destructive outbursts. What then? We have to learn to live closely and intimately with the Dove of God, and we have to allow the love of God and the Spirit of Christ to completely penetrate and permeate our lives so that we are people who speak only out of love for those around us. Then, our words will instead become incredibly constructive.

In the book of Proverbs, we find words like this:

> The tongue of the wise brings healing.
>
> A soft answer turns away wrath.

---

[94] R.W. Dale, *The Epistle of James and Other Discourses*, (Hodder & Stoughton, London, 1898), p.101

A gentle tongue is a tree of life.[95]

Whenever our hearts are 'dead in the water' and heavy with care, there are words that can give life and bring back a sense of hope. When our spirits are crushed and wounded, there are words that can bring healing. When our personal world is dry and exhausted, there are words that can refresh us.

Thought

Today, I am going to leash my tongue, and I am going to look for someone to whom I can bring a word of restorative grace.

Prayer

Jesus, let your Holy Spirit be the guiding factor and major influence over my speaking today.

---

[95] Prov.12:18b/15:1,4

DAY THIRTY-SIX

The Inconsistency of It All

3:9-12 (NLT)

Sometimes it praises our Lord and Father, and sometimes it curses those who have been made in the image of God. And so blessing and cursing come pouring out of the same mouth. Surely, my brothers and sisters, this is not right! Does a spring of water bubble out with both fresh water and bitter water? Does a fig tree produce olives, or a grapevine produce figs? No, and you can't draw fresh water from a salty spring.

Words are so important to us. R.W. Dale writes, "How wonderful a faculty speech is! It makes human society possible. Apart from words – visible or audible signs expressing inward thought and feeling – the inner life of man would be an island surrounded by an impassable sea."[96] Upon the good use of words, worlds are shaped, trust is built and the love of God is communicated. On the other hand, upon the evil use of words, worlds are destroyed, trust is demolished and the love of God is withheld.

As we continue with this letter, you begin to get the feeling that James really hates inconsistency. It seems to be a theme for him. (1:6-8/2:4) Here, in this passage, he is talking about the inconsistency of the tongue. John Bunyon, in his famous book 'Pilgrim's Progress', has a character called 'Talkative'. He is described as "a saint abroad and a

---

[96]   R.W. Dale, *The Epistle of James and Other Discourses*, (Hodder & Stoughton, London, 1898), p.99

devil at home"[97]. Isn't it true that we can sing intimate and powerful worship songs on a Sunday morning, and then go out and trash people over the Sunday lunch table? Isn't it true that we can pray moving prayers in the prayer meetings and then be crabby and impatient with those nearest to us? And the change can come within a moment...

J. A. Motyer, in his commentary, points out that it is not so much the inconsistency of blessing and cursing coming out of the same mouth as it is that both are aimed at the same object. When we bless and curse one, we bless and curse the other. Let me explain. James, you see, is telling us that we are all made in the image of God. Sin did not destroy that; it only stained and masked it. Hebrew thinking was that if you blessed your neighbour, you blessed God. Conversely, if you cursed your neighbour, you were cursing God. The fact of the matter is that we are all made in his image, and that is the point that James is seeking to put over here. The issue is that it's as if God was saying, "You touch my child, and you touch me. You rubbish my son or daughter, and you rubbish me." Or as the Italian version of God would have it, "You toucha him and you toucha ma face!"

James gives a few comparisons in the text: blessing and cursing, fresh and salt water. He talks of the incongruity of fig trees producing olives and a grapevine producing figs. In the middle of these, he gives a very strong word. "These things ought not to be so." This phrase is found only here in the Bible and the Greek is the strongest possible. One can translate it, "It's just not right!" Such inconsistency is unpalatable to the kingdom of God. It is totally out of place. Such things actually shock and grieve the Holy Spirit of God.

Jesus made the comment that we would be judged by every careless word that came out of our mouths. (Matt.12:36) He also said that out of the heart the mouth speaks. (Matt.12:34) Here is a challenge. People can hear what we say in public, but what do we think in our heart? People can hear what we speak face to face, but what do we say behind their back? May what we say in public be the same as what is said in private. In Psa.139:1-4, we read:

> *O LORD, you have searched me and known me! You know when I sit down and when I rise up; you discern my thoughts from afar. You search out my path and my lying down and*

---

[97] John Bunyan, *The Pilgrim's Progress*, (Oxford University Press, London, 1966), p.203

are acquainted with all my ways. Even before a word is on my tongue, behold, O LORD, you know it altogether.

It is both helpful and challenging to know that God hears both – our words and our thoughts.

Thought

In relationships, consistency breeds confidence and trust; inconsistency results in lack of confidence and distrust. Can we be trusted?

Prayer

Dear Lord, you hear my spoken words and you read my unspoken thoughts. Help me to continually bring them into line with each other.

DAY THIRTY-SEVEN

A Beautiful Life

3:13 (ESV)

Who is wise and understanding among you? By his good conduct let him show his works in the meekness of wisdom.

Everybody is looking for a new angle on things, a new way of presenting the truth that we believe in. In one sense, there is nothing wrong with that, because both language and culture changes. If we are seeking to accurately connect with our society, then we need to look at how we present things. If, however, we are pandering to this 'easily bored' spirit that is pervading our society, then I believe that we are on a wrong ticket.

Speaking against pretensions to originality, Dean Austin Farrar wrote, "There is nothing new to say on the subject, only the fashions of speech alter, and ancient argument is freshly phrased."[98] For those who are insistent that they have new revelation, then heed some good and humbling advice given to Bible students: if you arrive at an interpretation of Scripture that has not been noticed in the whole of our Christian history, then there is a high chance that you are wrong!

Gordon Fee and Douglas Stuart, in their seminal book, 'How to Read the Bible for All Its Worth', wrote:

Let it be said at the outset – and repeated throughout, that the aim of good interpretation is not uniqueness; one is not

---

[98] Austin Farrar, cited by Eugene Peterson, introduction to *Subversive Spirituality*, (Eerdmans. Michigan, 1997), p.ix

trying to discover what no one else has seen before ... unique interpretations are usually wrong.[99]

Having said all that, I personally love the unpacking of the meanings of words. By taking the time in discovering what the words actually mean in the original languages, we can often be treated to a feast; we can stumble into vistas sometimes indescribable. Both the Hebrew and Greek languages are so powerfully intensive and descriptive, that the English translations at times do not do them credit. It was J.B. Phillips who said, concerning translating the Greek into English:

> *It was like trying to rewire an ancient house without being able to switch off the mains, which was quite a vivid and modern metaphor, I hope. I got that feeling, the whole thing was alive, even while I was translating.*[100]

David said in Psa.119:130:

> *The unfolding of your words gives light; it imparts understanding to the simple.*

The word "unfolding" is the word 'pêthach', and it means 'an opening, an unfolding, an entrance, a doorway'. This speaks to me of the skill of an exegete – one who is able to dig out the true meaning of a verse or a text. This also speaks of the power of revelation by the Holy Spirit. Eugene Peterson puts it like this in the Message:

> *Break open your words; let the light shine out, let ordinary people see the meaning.*

Commentating on this passage, the NIVBC[101] says, "This passage is a natural outgrowth of the discussion of the tongue." In the previous section above we have James teaching the church about 'words' – in this section we have his teaching on 'works'. But holding it all together is our good conduct, which needs to be the source of both our words

---

[99] Gordon Fee and Douglas Stuart, *How to Read the Bible for All Its Worth*, (Scripture Union, Bletchley, 1993), pp.13,14

[100] *Translating the Gospels, A Discussion Between Dr. E.V. Rieu and the Rev. J.B. Phillips,* retrieved from http://www.bible-researcher.com/rieu.html

[101] *NIV Bible Commentary, Vol.2,* (Hodder & Stoughton, London, 1994), p.1031

and our works. How we live is of far more importance than what we say or what we do. Whatever is residing in our hearts will manifest itself in the things we say and how we say them, and also in our actions. The Expanded Translation by Kenneth Wuest captures it well:

> *Let him demonstrate from the source of a good and beautiful manner of life his works in meekness which is characterised by wisdom.*

In all our desire to communicate the truths of the gospel clearly and accurately, let us make sure that the main focus is on how we live. It is this that is heard and seen rather than all the words we speak or the things that we do.

Thought

Jesus epitomized the beautiful life, not so much by the things he said and the things he did, but the way in which he spoke and acted. It was with gentle compassion. It was with profound love.

Prayer

Jesus, may your Spirit embed more of your life in me today as I walk out into my world this day.

DAY THIRTY-EIGHT

The Two Wisdom Words

As we get into the passage today, we have this opening rhetorical question: "Who is wise and understanding among you?" These are the two wisdom words.

The first word is 'sophos', and it describes someone who is skilled and expert in his trade, like an inventor or a craftsman. It describes one who is wise and skilled in letters, someone who is cultivated and learned. It describes someone who can shape the best plan and use the best means to see it executed. This word is a technical word used by the Jews to describe the teacher, the scribe or the rabbi.

In the New Testament the Greek word 'sophos' is used firstly in the original classical sense to describe someone who is 'skilled in handicraft'. Secondly, the word describes someone who is 'accomplished in letters or learned'. Thirdly, it speaks in a practical sense, of 'the practice of the law of piety and honesty', of 'walking circumspectly'; and it is also represented as 'the quality adopted to adjust any differences in the church' – an aptitude much needed! In the higher, philosophical sense, the word speaks of 'devising the best counsels, and employing the best means to carry them out'. The NIVBC makes an interesting comment when it says:

> *James is still speaking to those who would be teachers (3:1); here it is not what they say he is concerned with, but rather how they live.*[102]

The best rendering would be "practical wisdom in godly living".

The second word is 'epistēmōn', and it describes someone who is intelligent, experienced, having the knowledge of an expert. The word

---

[102] *NIV Bible Commentary, Vol.2,* (Hodder & Stoughton, London, 1994), p.1031

describes a teacher, an expert in certain fields. James is saying such a person should possess knowhow and be skilled in the application of the truth to practical, everyday living. Peterson, in his introduction to the letter of James in the Message Bible, says:

Wisdom is not primarily knowing the truth, although it certainly includes that; it is skill in living.[103]

The wisdom of God is thoroughly practical. Wisdom must never become something esoteric, intended for, or understood by, only a small number of people with a specialized knowledge. Wisdom is not a secret language spoken and understood by a few academics to the exclusion of the man in the street, or in the pew.

I truly believe that it is the way we live, as human beings among other human beings, that gives an authenticity or otherwise to our testimony. The New Testament itself was written in 'koinē' or 'common' Greek, because God wanted all and sundry to understand his ways. In other words, the wisdom of God desires to find a home in an open, honest and clean heart. It is never primarily a matter of human intelligence or prowess. The wisdom of God is characterised by meekness. Let us, therefore, live humbly and rightly with each other so that others around us can see the wisdom of God manifested in us.

Thought

In Hebrew thought, God himself was to be sought after. After that, wisdom was the one thing to be chased after, and with a holy passion!

The beginning of wisdom is this: Get wisdom, and whatever you get, get insight.[104]

Prayer

Dear God, grant me not the clever and transient wisdom of this world, but grant me the gentle and meek wisdom of heaven.

---

[103] Eugene Peterson, *The Message Bible*, (NavPress, Colorado Springs, 2002), p.2201
[104] Prov.4:7

114

DAY THIRTY-NINE

The Two Behavioural Words

3:14 (NLT)

But if you are bitterly jealous and there is selfish ambition in your heart, don't cover up the truth with boasting and lying.

This is the stuff that can be in our hearts. Behind our clever rhetoric, silver-tongued wisdom and even precise theology can lurk both conscious and subconscious agendas that are actually foul and destructive to the cause of Christ. In this verse we can identify two 'couplets'.

The first couplet is "bitter jealousy". The word "jealousy" is 'zēlos', and it describes an 'excitement of mind, an ardour; a fervour of spirit in the embracing, the pursuing, or the defending of anything'. It is 'zeal in behalf of, for a person or thing'. It carries a sense of 'the fierceness of indignation or punitive zeal'. The Jewish nation make much of Phinehas, who, by his fierce jealousy for the honour of the Lord, slew two people who were openly rebelling against God's law.[105] He was the hero of 'the Zealots' found in the New Testament. It also speaks of 'an envious and contentious rivalry' that is more concerned with the point than with the person.

It is necessary to see the kind of jealousy that is spoken of here, because there is a right kind and also a wrong kind. God is jealous, but it is the right kind of jealousy.

---

[105] See Num.25:6-13

For you shall worship no other God, for the Lord whose Name is Jealous, is a jealous God.[106]

I love the rendering found in the NLT:

You must worship no other gods, for the LORD, whose very name is Jealous, is a God who is jealous about His relationship with you.

Paul was jealous when, in writing to the Corinthians, he said:

I feel a divine jealousy for you, since I betrothed you to one husband, to present you as a pure virgin to Christ.[107]

In the context of the verse in James, however, the word "jealous" is qualified by the word "bitterly". It is translated from the adjective 'pikros', which means 'bitter, harsh, or virulent'. It can carry the idea of 'piercing', in that it is 'cutting' to those who are on the receiving end.

The second couplet is "selfish ambition". It is, in fact, one word in the original text, 'eritheia', and it means 'strife, contention, or contentiousness'. It also means 'rivalry, electioneering or intriguing for office'. In the New Testament, it carried a sense of 'a courting of favour or distinction; a desire to put one's self forward; a partisan and fractious spirit'. This word is found before New Testament times only in Aristotle where it denotes a self-seeking pursuit of political office by unfair means. Paul talked of those who preached Christ out of 'eritheia'. (Phil.1:17) Dr Wayne Steury describes it as "having selfishness or self-promoting in your heart"[108].

Paul countered this kind of spirit by encouraging believers to "do nothing from selfish ambition or conceit, but in humility count others more significant than yourselves". (Phil.2:3) This is a 'not putting yourself forward or being selfish'. Again, there is a right and wrong kind of ambition; as followers of Christ, we make it our ambition, our aim and goal in life, to please him. (2.Cor.5:9) We aspire, we aim, we have as our ambition to live quietly, to mind our own affairs, and to work with our hands, that we might walk properly before outsiders and be dependent on no one. (1.Thess.4:11)

---

106 Ex.34:14
107 2.Cor.11:2
108 Wayne Steury, comment on *eritheia*, retrieved from http://classic.net.bible.org/strong.php?id=2052

The poet George Herbert (1593-1633) gave some excellent advice:

> *Be calm when arguing, because fierceness makes an error a fault, and it makes truth discourtesy. Why should I feel another man's mistakes more than his sicknesses or poverty? In love I should feel his mistakes as I would his sickness or his poverty; but anger is not love, nor wisdom neither; therefore, gently move.*[109]

Thought

An ambition that climbs over, disregards and hurts other individuals is totally incongruent with the ways of the kingdom of heaven. We are either serving Christ and each other, or we are serving ourselves.

Prayer

Dear Lord, never let my desire to be right override my love and relationships with those around me.

---

[109] George Herbert, The Temple, *The Church-porch*, retrieved from http://www.ccel.org/h/herbert/temple/27a.html

DAY FORTY

The Two Parentheses

3:13,16 (ESV)

Who is wise and understanding among you? By his good conduct let him show his works in the meekness of wisdom ... For where jealousy and selfish ambition exist, there will be disorder and every vile practice.

Today, we will look at the two parentheses that will give us further insight on what godly wisdom really is like and also on what selfishness can produce.

Firstly, we have the quality of wisdom. There is an authentic ring about the wisdom of God whereby you can easily recognise the sound of it. It is encapsulated in this little phrase: "the meekness of wisdom". The word "meekness" is 'prautēs', and the word basically means 'a mildness of disposition, a gentleness of spirit'. This word, however, needs to be qualified. The NIVBC says:

> *It is not a passive gentleness growing out of weakness or resignation; rather, it is an active attitude of deliberate acceptance. The word was used to describe a horse that had been broken and trained to submit to the bridle. So this gentleness is strength under control, the control of the Spirit of God.*[110]

This kind of wisdom is self-disciplined. Proverbs tells us that "a fool gives full vent to his spirit, but a wise man quietly holds it in".

---

[110] *NIV Bible Commentary, Vol.2,* (Hodder & Stoughton, London, 1994), p.1031

(Prov.29:11) The wisdom of God does not have to exert itself to be felt.

Then we have the fruit of selfishness, and that is seen in "disorder and every vile practice". The Expanded Translation calls it "restlessness, instability and every base deed". The Greek word translated "disorder" is 'akatastasia', which means 'a state of disorder, instability, disturbance, or confusion'. This is what selfishness produces in church life. Words that are spoken unwisely can unsettle things, whereas words that are spoken in gentle wisdom can bring harmony and stability. Things are known by their fruit, and it is often in the reaction to words, or the effect that they have, by which we recognize whether they are the wisdom of God or not. It is what we leave in our wake that tells everything about us.

The phrase "every vile practice" is better translated "every worthless practice". These are deeds that produce nothing in church life, and where things come to a standstill. Albert Barnes comments:

> ...of the truth of this no one can have any doubt who has observed the effects in a family or neighbourhood where a spirit of strife prevails. All love and harmony of course are banished; all happiness disappears; all prosperity is at an end. In place of the peaceful virtues which ought to prevail, there springs up every evil passion that tends to mar the peace of a community. Where this spirit prevails in a church, it is of course impossible to expect any progress in divine things; and in such a church any effort to do good is vain.[111]

Eugene Peterson puts it like this:

> Whenever you're trying to look better than others or get the better of others, things fall apart and everyone ends up at the others' throats.[112]

If the Holy Spirit is like a dove, then heed this little line: "The Spirit, like a peaceful dove, flies from the realms of noise and strife."[113] We need to so live that he is comfortable among us.

---

[111] Albert Barnes, *Notes on the Whole Bible,* commenting on Jas.3:16, e-sword.net
[112] The Message
[113] Isaac Watts, *Now by the Bowels of My God*

Thought

The proverb says that "a word fitly spoken is like apples of gold in a setting of silver". (Prov.25:11) A 'fitly spoken word' is a word that constructs and moves thing along, adding to and inspiring any conversation. Do my words do that, or do they deconstruct and bring the conversation to a jarring stop?

Prayer

Father, may my words today carry the healing and compassionate Spirit of God, who is ever seeking to build, restore and beautify our lives.

DAY FORTY-ONE

The Two Sources of Wisdom

3:14-16 (NLT)

...if you are bitterly jealous and there is selfish ambition in your heart, don't cover up the truth with boasting and lying. For jealousy and selfishness are not God's kind of wisdom. Such things are earthly, unspiritual, and demonic. For wherever there is jealousy and selfish ambition, there you will find disorder and evil of every kind.

We come now to look at the two sources of wisdom that are here contrasted in the text. Firstly, there is the wisdom of this earth. According to the NIVBC, this kind of wisdom "evaluates everything by worldly standards and makes personal gain life's highest goal"[114]. Paul says that God has actually "made foolish the wisdom of the world". (1.Cor.1:20) He goes on to say that "we do impart wisdom, although it is not a wisdom of this age or of the rulers of this age". (1.Cor.2:6) In other words, unlike the temporary, fluctuating and developing wisdom of this world and age, God's wisdom comes out of eternity, and it has never been modified, either by time or by human experience. God has not grown wiser over time. God's wisdom that he imparts is not a developed wisdom, it is not a learned wisdom, but it is a revealed wisdom. And what he reveals has neither been adapted to our times nor our circumstances.

---

[114] *NIV Bible Commentary, Vol.2*, (Hodder & Stoughton, London, 1994), p.1031

Interestingly, Charles Bridges (1794-1869) writes:

> *Earthly wisdom is gained by study; heavenly wisdom is gained by prayer. Study may form a biblical scholar, but prayer puts the heart under a heavenly tutelage.*[115]

James gives this kind of wisdom three characteristics. Firstly, it is "earthly". The Greek word here is 'epigeios', and it means 'that which is existing upon the earth, earthly, terrestrial'. It is earthly both in its source as well as its kind. The NIVBC says that "it views life from the limited viewpoint of this world rather than from heaven's vantage point"[116].

The second characteristic is that it is "unspiritual", or sensual. The Greek word here is 'psuchikos', and it means 'of or belonging to breath, having the nature and characteristics of the breath, the principal of animal life, which men have in common with animals'. It also means 'the sensuous nature with its subjection to appetite and passion'. It is the soul of man, operating without the energizing, purifying Spirit of God. Jude confirms all this by saying, "...it is these who cause divisions, worldly people ['psuchikoi'], devoid of the Spirit." (Jude 19)

The third characteristic is that it is "demonic". The Greek word here is 'daimoniōdēs', and it means 'something resembling or proceeding from an evil spirit'. This sounds quite harsh, until we examine what Jesus said when Peter tried to dissuade him from going to the cross. Jesus replied to him:

> *Get behind me, Satan! You are a hindrance to me. For you are not setting your mind on the things of God, but on the things of man.*[117]

The Jamieson, Fausset and Brown commentary added this note concerning Peter's restraining 'word of wisdom':

> *...for He felt in it a Satanic lure, a whisper from hell, to move Him from His purpose to suffer. So He shook off the Serpent, then coiling around Him, and 'felt no harm'. How quickly has the 'rock' turned to a devil! The fruit of divine*

---

[115] Charles Bridges, *A Commentary on Proverbs*, (The Banner of Truth Trust, Edinburgh, 1977), p.14

[116] *NIV Bible Commentary, Vol.2*, (Hodder & Stoughton, London, 1994), p.1031

[117] Matt.16:23

teaching the Lord delighted to honour in Peter; but the mouthpiece of hell, which he had in a moment of forgetfulness become, the Lord shook off with horror.[118]

These three characteristics – earthly, unspiritual, and demonic – answer to the three spiritual foes of man – the world, the flesh, and the devil – all of them hostile to the things of God. We must understand, too, and remember, that the tongue is the hardest member in our body to bring under control. Let us make sure then, that when we speak, we speak in the Holy Spirit of God.

Thought

The eternal wisdom of God is always relevant simply because it issues from a divine perspective. Don't be earthbound in your thinking.

Prayer

Dear Lord, please replace the earthly wisdom that so often seeks to instruct me with your heavenly wisdom that will transform me. Let me think your thoughts.

---

[118] *Jamieson, Fausset and Brown commentary,* commenting on Matt.16:23, e-sword.net

DAY FORTY-TWO

Pure, Peaceful and Gentle

3:17-18 (ESV)

But the wisdom from above is first pure, then peaceable, gentle, open to reason, full of mercy and good fruits, impartial and sincere. And a harvest of righteousness is sown in peace by those who make peace.

We have now looked a little in depth at aspects of this eternal wisdom of God as contrasted with the transient wisdom of this earth. God's wisdom is never out of date, and it is noted more for its Christ-like character than its incisive and spectacular content.

Now we want to major on the wisdom that comes from above. This wisdom is not cultivated as such, but it is received. It is not natural, but it is very supernatural; it is not studied for; rather, it is graciously and freely given to those who ask. James writes:

If any of you lacks wisdom, let him ask God, who gives generously to all without reproach, and it will be given him.[119]

It has very little to do with the capacity of the mind, but it has everything to do with the state of the heart. God's wisdom, you see, is primarily a matter of the heart, and God's wisdom resides in the heart. It has eight characteristics, and because of their importance, we will look at them in detail, one by one.

---

[119] Jas.1:5

124

The first characteristic is that it is "pure". We must notice the word "first". The Greek word is 'prōton', and means 'first in rank and time'.[120] Vincent's Word Studies says:

> ...the idea is not first numerically, but first essentially ... [The word "first" is there] emphasizing its inner quality, pure, as distinguished from its outward expressions. The other qualities are secondary as outgrowths of this primary quality.[121]

Purity, then, is the first thing that we will sense about the wisdom of God, and it sets the scene for all the other characteristics. The Greek word translated "pure" is 'hagnos', and it means 'chaste, innocent, holy, and clean'. In other words, this pure wisdom from God is a wisdom that is not only pure in itself, but it also excites and stimulates purity, reverence and respect in us. It goes further: it encourages and shapes our thinking concerning God and others. There is something sacred and venerable about it. It is pure from carnality; it is chaste and modest. It is a word used to describe an unsullied virgin. It is a wisdom that is immaculately pure from every fault. According to Wuest's Expanded Translation, this wisdom is "essentially pure". The NIVBC says:

> The reference is not to sexual purity but to the absence of any sinful attitude or motive. It is the opposite of a self-seeking attitude.[122]

The second characteristic is "peaceable". The Greek word is 'eirēnikos', and it means 'peaceable, pacific, loving peace'. The wisdom of this world often has a jarring and destabilising effect, but this wisdom from above will bring a peacefulness with it. It is both peaceful in its source, and peaceful in its effect.

The third characteristic is "gentle". The Greek word is 'epieikēs', and it means that which is 'seemly or suitable'. It has been also translated "sweetly reasonable" (Expanded Translation by Kenneth Wuest), "Courteous" (Weymouth), "quiet gentleness" (Living Bible). Another translation puts it as "kindly" (Jerusalem Bible). In other

---

[120] *Robertson's Word Pictures,* e-sword.net
[121] *Vincent's Word Studies,* e-sword.net
[122] *NIV Bible Commentary, Vol.2,* (Hodder & Stoughton, London, 1994), p.1032

words, this wisdom of God doesn't barge in, knocking all other thinking aside as inferior to itself, but it takes the thoughts and feelings of others into consideration. Out of interest, in the Greek version of the Old Testament (LXX), the word is used to describe God's disposition as King. He is gentle and kind, but firm in his application of truth. What a model this is for us!

Thought

It is a good thing to think about the character of wisdom. Sharpness in our words of wisdom will cut and fragment things, whereas the pure, gentle and peaceful wisdom of God will cleanse, reassure and settle things.

Prayer

Dear Lord, may I be the carrier of this kind of wisdom into my world today, and may it bring a beautiful fruitfulness into the lives of those around me!

DAY FORTY-THREE

Reasonable, Merciful and Fruitful

When you open up these powerful Greek words, there are often 'treasures of thought' that come tumbling out. In my view, it is well worth the effort to unpack them. Too often, our Bible reading can be just skimming the surface for a little thought that will touch our hearts for the day. There's nothing wrong with that, but just a little underneath the surface, there are powerful truths that will open up incredible and breath-taking vistas to our souls. They yield to a little digging with perseverance.

Continuing from yesterday, the fourth characteristic is that of being "open to reason". The Greek word here is 'eupeithēs', and it is only used here in the New Testament. It means 'sweetly reasonable, easily obeying, and compliant'. This wisdom, in other words, is a submissive wisdom. This wisdom is open to, and will listen well to, the thoughts of others. It is happy and ready to yield. There is nothing stubborn or obstinate about it. The man or woman who exhibits this kind of wisdom is easily approachable, and with them you feel that there can always be a debate on an issue.

So often, however, we find ourselves at the mercy of an opinion that is prefaced by "God said…" In reality, that usually means that there is no debate allowed. If I feel that I have something from God or that I have a genuine and strong opinion on something, if it cannot be weighed and judged and debated by others, then I doubt very much its veracity and authenticity. Words that cannot be weighed are weightless; words that can be weighed are weighty.

The fifth characteristic is that of being "full of mercy". This word "mercy" is the Greek word 'eleos', and it describes a heart of kindness or goodness towards the downhearted and the afflicted. It is also joined with a desire to help them. This wisdom from God carries his compassion and mercy with it. There is nothing judgmental about it, but it is sympathetic, and it seeks to understand the viewed problem and alleviate it. Mercy, you see, looks behind the issues to find the real reason – and it is usually pain. There is nothing reactive and knee-jerking about this wisdom of God; it has a deep respect for the individual.

The sixth characteristic is that it is full of "good fruits". The Greek words are 'agathos karpos', and they mean 'fruit that is good to the taste'. It is held in sharp contrast to "every vile practice", which always leaves a bitter taste in the mouth. This wisdom is evidenced by the good fruit that it leaves scattered behind it. You can see evidences of goodness and wholesomeness in its trail, it leaves such a positive mark. You see, it is not by our words that we are known; it is by the fruit we produce. Jesus said that we would recognise the false by the fruit that it produces.[123]

I believe that we are called to walk through this world leaving behind us good traces – lives that have been helped, hearts that have been encouraged and situations that have been beautifully and gently resolved. The words that we speak, and the things that we do, should be a blessing and not a burden to those around us. There is somehow a lovely fragrance about the wisdom of God, and when we diligently seek it, and find it, letting it shape our own hearts, our thinking and consequently our speaking, people on the receiving end will themselves sense its fragrance. It will have just a positive, healing, fruitful and restorative effect.

Thought

What will we leave in our trail today? At the end of the day, will people be thanking God for the influence that we have had upon them, or will they be in pain?

Prayer

God, please make me a carrier of your healing and restorative words today. May my words result in people giving you thanks this evening.

---

[123] See Matt.7:15-20/Lk.6:43

DAY FORTY-FOUR

Impartial and Sincere

We will now finish off this series of meditations on the wisdom that comes from above. Hopefully, it has introduced a greater awareness in us that how we behave and speak with each other, often in the name of the Lord into the issues of the life of the kingdom, is very important to God. Our words and our contributions can be either destructive or helpful. We can settle stormy waters or we can further trouble them.

The seventh characteristic is "impartial". The Greek word is 'adiakritos', and it means 'without partiality, without dubiousness, ambiguity or uncertainty'. This Greek word is only found here in the New Testament, and it is very rare in classical Greek. This wisdom from God, therefore, is steady, fair, persistent, and unmistakable. It shows no favouritism, and it does not discriminate. It actually desires that everyone gets a fair hearing.

The eighth characteristic of the wisdom from heaven is that it is "sincere". Here the Greek word is 'anupokritos', and it means 'unfeigned, undisguised, or sincere.' It is in contrast to the word that Jesus used of the Scribes and Pharisees, 'hupokritos', which means 'play actor, or one who pretends'. The wisdom from above, therefore, does not have to pretend, but it is the genuine article. It is the real thing, having a ring of authenticity about it. When we come into contact with the wisdom of God, we know at once that it is healthily true.

James goes on to say that you can see the fruit of this kind of wisdom. The fruit of this wisdom of heaven is "a harvest of righteousness". Whereas the fruit of the wisdom of the earth is "disorder and every vile practice", this fruit is wholesome and life-giving. As we have already noted, Jesus said of false prophets that they would be identified by their fruits – the stuff that they leave behind in their wake. It's not what they have said so much, but the result of what they have said. It is the end result, or the harvest of their sowings. God looks, however, for a harvest of peace from people of peace who construct peace. (Matt.5:9) It's interesting to note that the phrase 'close friend' in Hebrew literally means 'the man of my peace'. There are some people in this world that as soon as you are in their company, you start to relax. That is the effect of a close friend. That is also the fruit of godly wisdom; people start to relax.

The NIVBC says:

> ...to raise a harvest of righteousness demands a certain kind of climate. A crop of righteousness cannot be produced in the climate of bitterness and self-seeking. Righteousness will grow only in a climate of peace; thus it must be sown by the peacemakers. Such persons not only love peace and live in peace but also strive to create conditions of peace.[124]

They have peace with God; they have peace with themselves; they have peace with their circumstances; and they have peace with others. Having received the peace of God, they live in peace and they introduce peace into whatever circumstances they find themselves in. So, may what we do and say today flow out of a good and beautiful life that reflects accurately the life of the Lord Jesus, who is himself the Prince of Peace. May we have a very good effect on others, introducing the wisdom of heaven into our conversations and discussions this day.

Thought

We do not want the wisdom of God for ourselves only; that is spiritually selfish. We seek the wisdom of God also to be a blessing to others, creatively beautifying their worlds.

Prayer

Dear Father, you have created so much beauty. Help me to do the same in the lives of those who are around me today.

---

[124] *NIV Bible Commentary, Vol.2,* (Hodder & Stoughton, London, 1994), p.1032

DAY FORTY-FIVE

The Genesis of Strife

4:1 (NLT)

What is causing the quarrels and fights among you? Don't they come from the evil desires at war within you?

By way of reminder, and also to give some context to what is coming, let me make two comments here. The first is that earthly wisdom has 'self' at the epicentre whilst heavenly wisdom has others at the epicentre. Secondly, jealousy and selfish ambition were found firstly in the heart of Lucifer, who has become the arch strategist of division and disharmony, both in the world and in the church. The conclusion of chapter three is all about the sowing of peace; in chapter four, however, James opens up with the issue of quarrelling.

We cannot blame Lucifer for everything. Often the blame should be laid on our own doorsteps. James comes up with the truth that the cause for so much conflict around us actually lies within ourselves. The two words that he uses, "quarrels" and "fights" are fairly synonymous. We would say "trouble and strife". It can be said that the first word describes a 'bigger picture' battle that is prolonged, and the second word describes a skirmish that is narrowed down to an issue, and comes suddenly. Remember, too, that James is talking to Christians here. This is not physical warfare with traditional weapons. Instead, the weapons used here are the tongue (a sharp sword) and a bad attitude.

The real root of such divisive behaviour, according to James, is self-centredness. He talks about the "evil desires" that are at war within us. There are two things to observe here. The first is that the words "evil desires" are translated from the single Greek word 'hēdonē', from which we get our word 'hedonism'. Hedonism has as its goal the unqualified and unrestricted pursuit of pleasure. The NASB actually translates the word as "pleasures", whereas the KJV gets to the bones of it by translating the word as "lusts". Now, before we start to get the idea that God is against pleasure, James is talking here about inordinate, uncontrolled, undisciplined pleasures or passions. God is certainly not against pleasure; he is, however, much against selfishness, and he is certainly against all lust. Lust is always on the take, whereas love is always on the give.

Incidentally, Jesus said that our spiritual life is choked by the cares and riches and pleasures (hēdonē) of life, and that spiritual fruit does not mature.[125]

The second thought is that these warring passions dwell within us. The Greek word used for "war" is 'strateuomai'. It carries within it the sense of encampment, and suggests that these passions are 'encamped' or 'entrenched' within us. It is also the word that forms the basis of our word 'strategy'. They are well dug in.

What does all this mean? Simply this: there are vast areas, deeply ensconced within us all, unconquered by the Spirit of God, that remain ungovernable and resistant to godliness. Every now and then, these little unruly encampments kick off under certain circumstances, and get us into trouble, with others and with God. And according to James (reading between the lines), these passions kick off because we have seen something that we haven't got and someone else has. Desires that are not under the control of the Spirit, the conscience and reason, can leap ahead and take us out of God's boundaries. James is strong about the strength of uncontrolled passions or desires. Frustrated desires can lead to murder. We may not use actual weapons, but we can voice our frustration in destructive ways, and, as one has said, "If looks could kill, the world would be knee-deep in corpses." Inner conflict becomes the source of outer conflict.

Thought

Unconquered and ungoverned areas within us are the source of much distress and defeat. Maybe we need to ask the Holy Spirit to do

---

[125] See Lk.8:14

a deep cleansing and to bring under his, and our, control certain troublesome areas of our lives.

Prayer

Dear Lord, please do a new work of divine invasion into the dark and shadowy areas of my life. Leave no stone unturned until all that is within me is subdued and firmly under the government of your kingdom.

DAY FORTY-SIX

The Power of Passions

4:2,3 (ESV)

You desire and do not have, so you murder. You covet and cannot obtain, so you fight and quarrel. You do not have, because you do not ask. You ask and do not receive, because you ask wrongly, to spend it on your passions.

Our passions or desires are very strong elements within all of us. They need to be under the controlling disciplines of the Holy Spirit and the Word of God, or else they can lead us outside the boundaries of God and get us into trouble. If we are honest with ourselves, we all have a number of entrenched areas of unruly and undisciplined desires within us that still remain resistant to the guiding principles of heaven.

There are three words that are used in this passage to describe three different strengths of desires. They are "passions", "desire" and "covet". The first one is a translation of the Greek word 'hēdonē', which we discussed yesterday, and from which we get the word 'hedonism'. The Bloomsbury Dictionary describes hedonism firstly as "a self-indulgent devotion to pleasure and happiness as a way of life" and secondly as "a philosophical doctrine that pleasure is the highest goal or the source of moral values".[126] It seems that the phrase 'whatever makes you happy' is the watchword of a hedonistic lifestyle.

The next word, "desire", describes "the setting of the heart, the turning of the heart and attention, the longing for something that you presently do not have". The third word, "covet", describes a heart that

---

[126] *The Bloomsbury English Dictionary*, (Bloomsbury Publishing PLC, London, 1999), p.865

is warming towards something desired, and then becoming enflamed with a jealous and zealous passion. Here, there is almost a *fixation* about something. All these things leapt out and kicked into action when King David, in a moment of inactivity and leisure, saw Bathsheba. He then embarked on a totally irrational course of action that brought adultery, deception and murder into his life, with savage consequences. We must never underestimate the power of still unconquered passions within us. William Barclay wrote:

> *The steps of the process are simple and terrible. A man allows himself to think something. The thing begins to dominate his thoughts; he finds himself dreaming of it when he sleeps. It begins to be what is aptly called a ruling passion.* [127]

James then goes on to write about two reasons why we do not receive what we desire. The first one is simply that we do not ask. The asking here refers to *prayer* – the asking of God.

> *Give me one hundred preachers who fear nothing but sin and desire nothing but God, and I care not a straw whether they be clergymen or laymen; such alone will shake the gates of hell and set up the kingdom of heaven on earth. God does nothing but in answer to prayer.* [128]

So wrote John Wesley. If we took that to heart, what might it do to our prayer lives? Maybe a lot more would happen among us if we did pray more.

The second reason for not receiving what we desire – and here it is still in the context of prayer – is that we ask "wrongly". The word is 'kakōs', and it describes something that is bad, rotten or corrupt. Here is yet another example of a biblical reason for unanswered prayer, and there are quite a few in the Scriptures. [129] It is therefore so essential that our motives in our prayers are good. Why are we praying the prayers we do? James is quite strong on this. If it is for selfish reasons, for personal self-indulgent pleasures, then we shall get short thrift from

---

[127] William Barclay, *The Letters of James and Peter,* The Daily Study Bible, (The St Andrew Press, Edinburgh, 1976), p.100

[128] John Wesley, cited by E.M. Bounds, *Power Through Prayer*, (Marshall Brothers Ltd, London), p.100

[129] See, for example, Psa.66:18/Isa.1:15/Jer.11:11-14/1.Pet.3:7

heaven. Remember, godly wisdom has others at the epicentre, and so do godly desires. Recall also that God is not against pleasure and happiness, but he does stand firm against selfishness and self-indulgence. The Message calls it "wanting your own way". Let us be giving in our interactions with others and giving in our prayers.

Thought

An unchecked and misshaped passion is dangerous to the soul, whereas a Spirit-fuelled and directed passion is most powerful and very effective.

Prayer

Lord, help me to bring my passion under the guidance and discipline of the Holy Spirit so that it may hit my God-given target.

DAY FORTY-SEVEN

Friendship with the World

4:4 (NLT)

You adulterers! Don't you realize that friendship with the world makes you an enemy of God? I say it again: If you want to be a friend of the world, you make yourself an enemy of God.

This is one of those shocking verses that we come across now and then in the Scriptures. It is shocking in that it stops us quite suddenly in our tracks and it tells us to reconsider everything about the way we are living. Here we see the clashing of cultures, ethics, perceptions and lifestyle.

James comes to us with a knockout blow: "You adulterous people!" (ESV) Whenever I read this, I am reminded of the words of Paul to the Corinthians. He wrote:

> *For I feel a divine jealousy for you, since I betrothed you to one husband, to present you as a pure virgin to Christ. But I am afraid that as the serpent deceived Eve by his cunning, your thoughts will be led astray from a sincere and pure devotion to Christ.*[130]

This is simply spiritual adultery, wanting to sleep in two beds, as it were. When we have another love in our life, other than Jesus, we are on the verge of spiritual adultery. He must be the number one love of our heart.

When James goes on to say, "Do you not know..." he uses what I call the 'revelation word' for knowing. It is 'iodate', which means 'to

---

[130] 2.Cor.11:2,3

see'. This kind of knowledge does not come from study or even experience, but it comes by God opening our eyes so that the spiritual penny drops. We have to see it, and see it clearly for ourselves: that friendship with the world leads to hostility with God.

What is this friendship with the world? Hear it in the Message: it is "flirting with the world every chance you get..." Now, this verse is not at all about being *relevant* to the world; it is all about whom we are in love with. If I am in love with Christ, then I want to take on board his values and his ways. If on the other hand, I want to take on board the values and ways of the world, then I am actually shunning Christ. Paul, in his letter to Timothy, laments the slipping away and desertion of a certain former colleague called Demas because he has fallen in love with the world. (2.Tim.4:10) Adamson writes that the two phrases "friendship with the world" and "enemy of God" are "both objective, conveying strongest ethical contrast". The way the Greek language is constructed here "conveys strong ethical contrast"[131]. In other words, the values and the ways of the world are, and always will be, completely antithetical to the kingdom of heaven. The apostle John wrote:

> *Do not love this world nor the things it offers you, for when you love the world, you do not have the love of the Father in you. For the world offers only a craving for physical pleasure, a craving for everything we see, and pride in our achievements and possessions. These are not from the Father, but are from this world.*[132]

Remember that the battle for our heart and soul is not always on the outside of us; it is also an inner war. Consider Rom.8:5-8 and Gal.5:16,17.

James says that friendship results in becoming God's "enemy". This is a very strong word. It is hatred or hostility. We do well to remember that the firstfruit of salvation is actually "peace" with God. (Rom.5:1) When we make a deliberate, purposeful and selfish choice to befriend the world's values and ways, we will find ourselves rendered at variance with heaven. Authentic Christianity has always been different. It always will be; and those who love the Lord with a sincere and pure

---

[131] James Adamson, *The Epistle of James*, (Eerdmans, Michigan, 1976), p.170
[132] 1.Jn.2:15-17 (NLT)

devotion will always find themselves on a collision course with the world we live in. John Bunyan's 'Mr Facing-both-ways' was a sickly parody of a half-hearted follower of Christ. Such a walk is listless, lifeless and a smack in the face of the Lord who gave his all for each one of us.

Thought

Who or what has the greatest tug on your heartstrings? Remember, God is a jealous lover.

Prayer

Dear Lord, you have my heart. It is yours, and I will not give it to another. All else, I will love and appreciate in your name, but they will never have the place that you do in my affections.

DAY FORTY-EIGHT

The Jealous Lover

4:5 (NLT)

Do you think the Scriptures have no meaning? They say that God is passionate that the spirit he has placed within us should be faithful to him.

Let's stay with this a little longer. James is being quite passionate here, and he is using strong words. He's talking about spiritual adultery, about friendship with the world both equalling and resulting in hatred or hostility toward God. Why is he so strong? What has gotten into his spirit? In my view, I think it is because he has picked up the heartbeat of God towards us. God is a jealous lover. Peterson has caught it in his rendering of the text. He writes:

And do you suppose God doesn't care? The proverb has it that 'he's a fiercely jealous lover'.[133]

In Exodus we read:

For I, the Lord your God, am a jealous God who will not share your affection for any other god.[134]

You must worship no other gods, but only the Lord, for he is a God who is passionate about his relationship with you.[135]

The bottom line is this: God has placed his Spirit within us, and he has caused our own spirit to be awakened and drawn into a deep and

---

[133] The Message
[134] Ex.20:5 (NLT)
[135] Ex.34:14 (NLT)

intimate union with him. In one sense, we have been 'wedded' to Christ, and now we share everything with him. Remember the words of Paul to the believers in Corinth:

> *For I feel a divine jealousy for you, since I betrothed you to one husband, to present you as a pure virgin to Christ.*[136]

We have been called out of the ways and values of this world in order to walk in the ways and values of his world. Let me give an accurate definition of what we mean by 'the ways and values of the world'. Archbishop Trench described it as:

> *...all that floating mass of thoughts, opinions, maxims, speculations, hopes, impulses, aims, aspirations at any time current in the world ... impossible to seize and accurately define, but which constitute a most real and effective power...*[137]

The Holy Spirit, through the gospel, has drawn us out and away from all that, and placed us in a kingdom where everything is new and the values and principles are totally different. Turning back and falling in love again with the ways and values of the world is spiritual adultery, and, I repeat, *God is a fiercely jealous lover.*

We cannot have it both ways. Scripture is full of admonitions about that all the way from Elisha's "limping between two different opinions" (1.Kgs.18:21) to Jesus saying, "You cannot serve God and money." (Matt.6:24) It's one or the other. We love God or we love the world. To love both is spiritual adultery. God is passionate about his relationship with you and me, and he hates anything or anyone who gets in the way of that relationship. The big question is, do we feel the same? Are we fiercely jealous over our relationship with him? There are lots of things, practices and values out there that will clamour for our attention and even our hearts. Let us therefore be absolutely determined in the maintaining of our love for him, just as he is with us. Let us be ruthless in letting nothing and no-one come between us.

---

[136] 2.Cor.11:2

[137] Archbishop Trench, cited in *Word Studies in the Greek New Testament, Vol.1,* by Kenneth Wuest, commentary on Ephesians and Colossians, (Eerdmans, Michigan, 2004), p.61

Thought

Jesus talked about the possibility of the seed of God that has been planted in us being "choked by the cares and riches and pleasures of life..." (Lk.8:14) Are there any weeds and thorns in the garden of your soul that need pulling out? Would you let the Lord show them to you?

Prayer

Dear Holy Father, please cast your eye over the garden of my soul, and point out to me anything that has received more attention in my affections than it should have.

DAY FORTY-NINE

The Greater Grace

4:6 (NLT)

And he gives grace generously. As the Scriptures say, "God opposes the proud but gives grace to the humble."

The great struggles in our Christian life are, as an ancient writer puts it, against "the world, the flesh and the devil". The first is a set of ways and values that surround us; the second is all that unconquered selfishness within us, and the third is a malevolent personality who uses both to cripple, stunt and divert our passionate love relationship with Christ.

The struggle is a very real one. Sometimes it is full on, and you know exactly what you are struggling against, and other times, it is quite insidious and subtle. Either way, Satan, the enemy of our souls, is determined to either wrench or wean us away from a pure devotion to the Lord.

But God always is more than a match for the many attempts to seduce us. James tells us that "he gives grace generously". The way this is phrased in Greek is better translated "he gives a far greater grace". Alec Motyer writes, "His resources are never at an end, his patience is never exhausted, his initiative never stops, his generosity knows no limit."[138] Paul concurs when he writes, "Where sin increased, grace abounded all the more..." (Rom.5:20) When Paul was once faced with a difficulty that was not going to go away, God said to him, "My grace is sufficient for you."

---

[138] J. A. Motyer, *The Message of James: The Message of James*, The Bible Speaks Today series, (IVP, Leicester, 1985), p.150

I love the Message here:

> *"My grace is enough; it's all you need. My strength comes into its own in your weakness." Once I heard that, I was glad to let it happen. I quit focusing on the handicap and began appreciating the gift.*

God always gives more than this life can offer us or throw at us.

James goes on to mention two opposites: the proud and the humble. He says that God opposes the former and gives to the latter. The words chosen here are not about those who are gifted and those who are not. This is all about attitudes, not abilities. It's talking about one's outlook on life, and also how one views others. Great ability with a bad attitude does not bless the Lord or his church. Great attitude with little ability is better, but the best is great attitude and great ability.

James taught that the Lord actually opposes the proud. The word that is used here is an old military word, and it means 'to range oneself against an enemy'. It means to take up a deliberate position in order to oppose and fight off any further movement. Those who have a proud outlook on life and others will find the Lord resisting and opposing them at every turn. So, if our way forward is being blocked, it may not be the enemy...

On the other hand, those with a humble outlook on life and others will find the Lord filling them up with good things. It's as if heaven will bend over backwards to help, assist and empower them. To them, God gives grace, that wonderful, door-opening, energy-giving, life-enthusing, ability-enabling, difficulty-defying, rising above, breaking-through dimension of God. Heaven is waiting to wonderfully and powerfully resource us as we keep our devotion to Christ pure and un-mixed, but will stand against us if we decide to cuddle up to someone or something else.

Thought

God has not left us to ourselves to muddle through as best as we can. Within us, and around us, and therefore available to us, are the unbelievably boundless stores of grace.

Prayer

Dear Lord, I stand amazed and humbled that you, and the resources of heaven, stand so near to me. Open my eyes!

DAY FIFTY

Stances of Faith

4:7,8 (ESV)

Submit yourselves therefore to God. Resist the devil, and he will flee from you. Draw near to God, and he will draw near to you. Cleanse your hands, you sinners, and purify your hearts, you double-minded.

God really hates pride, and he will set himself against it. But the devil loves it, thrives on it and indeed uses it. It first became apparent in Lucifer's heart right at the beginning of time, when he wanted to elevate himself above the throne of God.[139] The Greek word for "proud" is 'huperēphanos', which means 'to show oneself, or to appear to be above other people'. The bottom line is this: the moment we feel we are above others in any way, we have lost the spiritual plot. The apostle Paul is also quite clear on this when he writes to the Philippians, "...in humility count others more significant than yourselves." (Phil.2:3) I particularly like Eugene Peterson's rendering of this text in the Message:

> *Don't push your way to the front; don't sweet-talk your way to the top. Put yourself aside, and help others get ahead.*

James now gives us four things to do. The first is that we are to "submit [ourselves] to God". The Greek word that is translated "submit" is 'hupotassō', and it means 'to arrange ourselves under God'. You see, the antidote to pride is a deliberate stance of humility. Notice also that it is a corporate act; in other words, we do it together. There is no room for an independent spirit in the economy of God.

---

[139] See Isa.14:12-14

146

James Adamson translates it as "enlisting under God"[140]. It involves a corporate submission to his way of thinking and his way of doing things, and that needs an obedient heart. We have started to mature when we can do as we are told.

The second thing James tells us to do is to "resist the devil". This has a promise with it: "...he will flee from you!" The Greek word translated "resist" is 'anthistēmi', which means 'to take a stand against, to resist, and to oppose'. This is not passivity; rather, it is where we aggressively dig our heels in and refuse to let him have his way with us. Alec Motyer writes:

> *It is not a word for one who is carrying the attack over into the enemy camp, but for one who is manning the defences, knowing that enemy pressure is ceaseless and that he is constantly under fire.*[141]

James does not say, "Chase the devil..." Too many do that, and end up down foggy cul-de-sacs. A powerful word in our spiritual walk is 'no'.

Thirdly, James tells us to "draw near to God", and that too has a promise: "...he will draw near to you." The phrase originally came from the Old Testament High Priestly function of 'drawing near' to God. The rabbis also taught, "God goes out to those who approach him." Another thing to note here is that the text seems to suggest that we make the first move. We have to make the choice to approach him. God wants relationship with us, but he seems to say, "I have already made the biggest move; now it's your turn."

Lastly, James tells us to "cleanse [our] hands" and to "purify [our] hearts". At first this stood to mean ceremonial cleansing, but it became clear that God is looking for both an ethical and inner cleanliness. In the Old Testament, God looked for clean lips (Isa.6:5), clean hands (Psa.24:4) and a clean heart (Psa.73:13). In the New Testament, Jesus said that it was "the pure in heart [who] shall see God". (Matt.5:8) We need to actively disengage from what is ethically wrong, and we need

---

[140] James Adamson, *The Epistle of James*, The New International Commentary on the New Testament series, (Eerdmans, Michigan, 1976), p.174

[141] J. A. Motyer, *The Message of James: The Message of James*, The Bible Speaks Today series, (IVP, Leicester, 1985), p.152

to seek a pure and undivided attention to the Lord, knowing that he walks and talks with the humble and pure of heart.

Thought

When life revolves around me, somehow I am out of sync with heaven.

Prayer

Dear Lord, help me to see that I am not the most important person in the world.

DAY FIFTY-ONE

Speaking Against Each Other

4:11,12 (NLT)

Don't speak evil against each other, dear brothers and sisters. If you criticize and judge each other, then you are criticizing and judging God's law. But your job is to obey the law, not to judge whether it applies to you. God alone, who gave the law, is the Judge. He alone has the power to save or to destroy. So what right do you have to judge your neighbor?

One thing that I am learning, and re-learning, is that I have to let the Scriptures speak to me and inform me on every aspect of life. I must never superimpose my own theological bent or preferences into the text. This is not easy to do. We are all 'influenced' people one way or another – by our upbringing, by our church culture, by the books we read and also by the people we listen to. So, when we come to James, we have to let him talk to us, influence us, challenge us, and change, if necessary, our own paradigms and our ways of thinking.

James returns again to the sins of the tongue. He writes to prohibit the church speaking evil against each other. The word he chooses to use here is 'katalaleō', and it has a wide spectrum of meaning: 'criticising, devaluing, disparaging, censuring, belittling, talking down' to name but a few. J.B. Phillips translates, "...never pull each other to pieces..." It is all summed up in the phrase 'traducing', which is when we speak something critical or negative about someone or something.

The context of all this is that God is passionate about our relationship with him, and he is also just as passionate about our relationships with each other. In fact, I believe the Scriptures teach that when we belittle and malign a child of God, we are also belittling and maligning God his Father. The rabbis teach that when we do that, it causes the Shekinah glory to leave. In fact, Jesus taught us that the way we treat the least of our brothers is a reflection of how we actually treat him.

James teaches that when we speak evil about someone, we also make a judgment about that person. And unlike a court of law, we never have all the facts. We act and speak as prosecutor without giving room for the defence. The word "judge" used here means 'to separate, to pick out, and to distinguish from another'. In other words, when we criticise and judge someone, we mentally, emotionally and spiritually remove them from the team, setting them apart in order to pick on them, and make comment on how they are different from us. That's not a lot different from what Satan loves to do to us; and the trouble is, he loves to separate us in order to pull us down. Negative gossip is so seductive. Once it has gained entrance, it is very difficult to shift.[142]

James takes the argument further and says that when we do this to each other, we are making judgments on God's Law, and actually on the Lawgiver himself. So, if we feel that we have to make a negative comment on someone, then we are treating God's primary word to 'love our neighbour as we love ourselves' as of no consequence, and we are also treating God as being dilatory or inadequate, feeling that if he is silent, then we ought to speak up.

James finishes by saying, "Who are you to judge another?" Dr Martyn Lloyd-Jones used to say that if ever we saw the full extent of our own sinfulness, we would never point an accusing or critical finger at anyone else ever again. Let us determine, therefore, to start finding points of praise in each other.

Thought

See who is around you today, and determine to speak words of encouragement to them.

Prayer

Father, I have never known you to belittle me. Please let some of that great heart of yours influence mine.

---

[142] See Prov.26:22

DAY FIFTY-TWO

Leaving God Out of the Planning

4:13-17 (ESV)

Come now, you who say, "Today or tomorrow we will go into such and such a town and spend a year there and trade and make a profit" – yet you do not know what tomorrow will bring. What is your life? For you are a mist that appears for a little time and then vanishes. Instead you ought to say, "If the Lord wills, we will live and do this or that." As it is, you boast in your arrogance. All such boasting is evil. So whoever knows the right thing to do and fails to do it, for him it is sin.

In this next section, James continues his cautions against the wrong use of our tongue. Earlier he counselled against speaking ill of each other; here he counsels against speaking presumptuously, speaking as if God's plans and purposes did not matter or figure in our equations.

Alec Motyer talks of three areas of presumption that he feels James is addressing. Firstly, our everyday life – calling it our "today or tomorrow"; then he speaks of our choices – "we will go..."; and then he speaks of our abilities – "we will trade and make a profit..." He writes:

We speak as if life were our right. We speak as if our choice were the deciding factor. We speak as though we had the

ability to make ourselves succeed: the presumption that my
life belongs to me! That is what James is against.[143]

How do we guard against this kind of presumption? There are three little phrases that we need to take note of: "you do not know", "you are" and "you ought".

Firstly, James says that we need to recognise our ignorance. No-one knows what the future will bring. We speak of our future plans without knowledge. Jesus talked of a rich fool who projected well into the future but lost his life that night. Solomon wrote, "Do not boast about tomorrow, for you do not know what a day may bring."[144]

Secondly, we then need to recognise our frailty. We are not as substantial as we think. Biblically speaking, we are an insubstantial, transient mist or vapour that is around for a very short time. The psalmist wrote, "My days are like an evening shadow; I wither away like grass.' (Psa.102:11)

Finally, we need to recognise our dependence on God for our life and for our activities. James wrote, "You ought to say, if the Lord wills, we will live and do this or that." Today, a lot of people think that this is quite religious, but this is a perfectly biblical way of thinking. Paul says to the Corinthians, "I will come to you soon, if the Lord wills," (1.Cor.4:19) and, "I hope to spend some time with you, if the Lord permits." (1.Cor.16:7) In Acts 18:21, he says to the Ephesians, "I will return to you if God wills."

Presumption, then, manifests itself firstly as "a form of practical atheism"[145]. This is living our own lives with a "tint of faith" as one churchgoer once described herself. Then, secondly, it is simply human arrogance and boasting. Alec Motyer describes it as:

...an element of the proud, boasting, human spirit that
vaunts its independence ... Genesis 3 reveals that this is the
sin of Eden, the determination of man to be master of his

---

[143] J. A. Motyer, *The Message of James: The Tests of Faith*, (IVP, London, 1970), p.94

[144] Prov.27:1

[145] James Adamson, *The Epistle of James*, (Eerdmans, Michigan, 1976), p.179

own destiny, steer his own life and rest upon his own ability to be his saviour. It is evil.[146]

James is actual saying to us, "When you think of the future, don't leave God out of the planning, but put him in the forefront of it all." Don't brag about what we will accomplish tomorrow; we might not be here tomorrow. As one proverb puts it:

Many are the plans in the mind of a man, but it is the purpose of the LORD that will stand.[147]

James then finishes with the presumptuous 'sin of omission'. In other words, don't treat this exhortation as of little importance. Failing to do what we now know to be right is sinful. This is a key principle of the spiritual life – we learn what is right and we then start to practise it. It is always the practitioners, rather than the knowers, of truth who are blessed of God.

Thought

We humans keep brainstorming options and plans, but GOD's purpose prevails.[148]

Do we want God to follow us, and bless our plans? Or is it that we are meant to be following him?

Prayer

Dear Lord, forgive me for the times I have meticulously made plans without involving you. Help to remedy that from today.

---

[146] J. A. Motyer, *The Message of James: The Tests of Faith*, (IVP, London, 1970), p.96
[147] Prov.19:21
[148] Prov.19:21 (MSG)

DAY FIFTY-THREE

A Warning to the Plutocrats

5:1-6 (NLT)

Look here, you rich people: Weep and groan with anguish because of all the terrible troubles ahead of you. Your wealth is rotting away, and your fine clothes are moth-eaten rags. Your gold and silver are corroded. The very wealth you were counting on will eat away your flesh like fire. This corroded treasure you have hoarded will testify against you on the day of judgment. For listen! Hear the cries of the field workers whom you have cheated of their pay. The cries of those who harvest your fields have reached the ears of the Lord of Heaven's Armies. You have spent your years on earth in luxury, satisfying your every desire. You have fattened yourselves for the day of slaughter. You have condemned and killed innocent people, who do not resist you.

Looking at this passage today, I'm not sure that many of us would sit easy if James was the pastor of our church. He has such a passion for spiritual integrity that he writes, at times, like a scathing Old Testament prophet. A true and passionate love for God will most definitely equate with a scathing hatred for sin and spiritual pretentiousness.

So, who is James attacking here? J.B. Phillips feels that he is addressing the plutocrats; in other words, the wealthy ruling class, the big employers. Most scholars actually feel that he is also addressing both the unconverted and the converted here. It could well be directed at those who were trying to combine God and high finance in their lives at the cost of others. Let's be clear about this: wealth is often viewed as the blessing of God. It was Moses who taught that it is God who gives us the power or ability to get wealth.[149] The big issues, however, are our attitudes and what we do with our wealth. It is not money that is the root of all evil. That actually is a misquote. It is "the *love* of money" that is a root of "all kinds of evils".[150] One of the bad effects of wealth is that it can tend to create a moral and spiritual complacency.

James, then, levels his onslaught at four activities. Firstly, these plutocrats were hoarding their wealth. Wealth is the abundance of possessions, but they were in love with their possessions far too much. The main manifestation of selfishness, in fact, is the desire to possess, and to possess more.

Secondly, they were not paying the labourers their wages. In biblical days, wages were usually paid on a daily basis. In today's business world, the withholding of payment in order to gain more interest at the bank is very much akin to this kind of treatment. Adamson notes that "unlike the slave, who had someone who might protect his interests, the free labourer had none"[151]. They could easily get ripped off.

Then, thirdly, they were living in self-indulgent luxury. The two words used here are synonyms, although there is a shade of difference. One speaks of an enervating or weakening 'softness of life' and the other speaks of an extravagant wastefulness. Both have the effect of the weakening of morals and spiritual sharpness.

Lastly, James addresses the callous murder of helpless innocents. Adamson writes:

> ...the rich are represented, not as bold and fearless champions, defending a cause against dangerous enemies, but as brutal bullies, picking as the victims of the outrages those who either cannot or will not resist.[152]

To these plutocrats, James speaks a severe judgment: all their hoarded treasures are going to decay, and it is that very decay that will eventually condemn them. He actually calls upon them to "weep and

---

[149] See Deut.8:18
[150] 1.Tim.6:10
[151] James Adamson, *The Epistle of James*, (Eerdmans, Michigan, 1976), p.186
[152] Ibid, p.188

groan" because life is going to become very miserable for them. The word translated "groan" ("howl" in the ESV) is the Greek word 'ololuzō', and it is used only here. It is an onomatopoeic – a word that sounds like a howl. It actually is a howl of grief. God's anger against the abuse of the poor and downtrodden will one day erupt against those who abuse them. And I, for one, would not like to be in their shoes or anywhere near them when it does.

Thought

Jesus said, "Life is not measured by how much you own."[153]
How do you measure yours?

Prayer

How about the prayer of Agur:

O God, I beg two favours from You; let me have them before I die. First, help me never to tell a lie. Second, give me neither poverty nor riches! Give me just enough to satisfy my needs. For if I grow rich, I may deny You and say, "Who is the LORD?" And if I am too poor, I may steal and thus insult God's holy name.[154]

---

[153] Lk.12:15 (NLT)
[154] Prov.30:8,9 (NLT)

DAY FIFTY-FOUR

Be Patient

5:7-8 (ESV)

Be patient, therefore, brothers, until the coming of the Lord. See how the farmer waits for the precious fruit of the earth, being patient about it, until it receives the early and the late rains. You also, be patient. Establish your hearts, for the coming of the Lord is at hand.

In the previous passage, James had rounded on the ruling wealthy plutocrats that were probably connected to the congregation. He had accused them of hoarding their wealth and of abusing the poor. Now, it seems, he turns his attention to those very poor who are also part of the congregation. These next few verses are linked to the previous passage by the word "therefore". He is saying, "Be patient, for a day is surely coming when injustices and abuses shall be looked at, dealt with and put right."

We know that the Lord is coming, and when He does, each man will have to answer to him. The word "coming" is the Greek word 'parousia', and it means 'presence'. In other words, the Lord himself will come and make his presence known and felt.

James tells them to be "patient", and that word is mentioned three times here. The word is rooted in the lovely Greek word 'makrothumia', and it has a wealth of meaning. It literally means to be 'longsuffering'.

It is a patient holding out under trial; a long-protracted restraint of the soul from yielding to passion, especially the passion of anger.[155]

The appeal is to the oppressed brethren. Catch your wind for a long race (long-tempered as opposed to short-tempered).[156]

The illustration given is that of a farmer, patiently waiting for a precious harvest. He has tilled the land and sown the seed, and now he has to wait. There is nothing to do except wait. He knows with a certainty that the harvest will eventually come. In like manner, says James, we have this certain hope of his coming, with a certain harvest of both salvation and judgment. The mention of the two rains is significant. The early rains soften the soil for sowing and germination, and the latter rain swells the head of grain for harvesting. Incidentally, Alec Motyer sees both rains as buffeting storms, not gentle, refreshing drizzles. The buffeting rains are very productive. Thinking spiritually, God has designed storms as well as sunshine for the shaping of our souls.

James goes on to tell them to "establish [their] hearts". J.B Phillips puts that as "resting your heart on the ultimate certainty"[157]. The word "establish" comes from a word which means 'to stabilize, to fix and to strengthen'. Our hearts can beat wildly at times, and run all over the place when under pressures and things are not right. This stabilising of the heart is set in contrast with the 'fattening' of the heart in verse 5. A stabilised heart is a focused and settled heart; a fattened heart, on the other hand, is insensitive and cannot feel the prodding finger of the Lord.

We stabilise our heart by nailing it to certain truths. In this instance, Christ is coming again, and on that day all wrongs will be righted. In the meanwhile, however, be patient, learn how to wait and work in tandem with God and his timings – knowing what you can and cannot do – and persevere restfully right on to the end. Pin your hope on him.

---

[155] *Vincent's Word Studies,* e-sword.net
[156] *Robertson's Word Pictures,* e-sword.net
[157] The Message

Thought

Patience is not a gift to be received; it is a virtue to nourish and grow.

Prayer

Dear Father, please forgive me for the impatience that so quickly rises up within me when I find myself under pressure to react. Help me to transform my frustrations into a restful and trusting spirit.

DAY FIFTY-FIVE

Patience and Impatient

5:9 (NLT)

Don't grumble about each other, brothers and sisters, or you will be judged. For look – the Judge is standing at the door!

Let's stay with this a little longer. Waiting does not come easy for most of us, and especially when we are under pressure. James was addressing this in the church by encouraging patience under pressure. The unspoken (and even the spoken) phrase "Hurry up!" is close to all of us. The biblical word 'patience' is, however, an exercise in a long and sustained keeping of the soul in inner peace, not allowing oneself to get inwardly and outwardly rattled in any way.

This particular verse comes as a bit of a parenthesis to the passage. James tells the pressured and beleaguered believers to refrain from grumbling. The word is 'stenazō', and means 'to sigh or to groan'. It speaks of those deep, subterranean feelings of dissatisfaction and resentment that do not actually get voiced, but they come out with a sigh or a groan. Many times, an optimistic atmosphere has been killed by such a sigh. Words have not been spoken, but a noise has been made, and it has drained off any peace or faith that may have been present. We must never underestimate the power of a sigh. We may feel it has done us good to vent our frustrations, but it never produces anything positive – rather, it takes the life and heart away from those in the immediate vicinity. Matthew Henry says that it introduces unease among us.[158] And God hates it.

---

[158] See Matthew Henry, *Commentary on the Whole Bible*, (Marshall, Morgan and Scott, London, 1960), p.735

Notice, too, that it is not a groaning so much against adverse or difficult circumstances, but rather against fellow believers. It is levelled at the one who has 'let us down', or who has 'fallen short of our expectations'. James is quite clear here: when we do such a thing, we have actually made a judgment. We have set up a level, or a standard, and when that is not met, then we become frustrated and we sigh.

So, whenever we do make a critical judgment about another believer, we actually set up a standard. It is *our* standard, it is the way *we* see things, but it is also the standard that God will then take and use as a framework by which to judge us. There is a principle to be found in the Scriptures that as we treat others, so God will treat us, and often allow others to treat us. If God has freely forgiven me, and is so tolerant and patient with me, then that ought to be reflected in the way I view and treat others. Thomas à Kempis wrote:

> *Try to bear patiently with the defects and infirmities of others, whatever they may be, because you also have many a fault which others must endure.*[159]

James says that the Judge himself is standing at the door. It is he who sees our heart, and listens to not only our words that we speak behind closed doors, but also our unspoken thoughts and our sighs. He will talk to us about them. He could be at the door right now listening and observing. He could be about to return in the middle of our conversation. James instructs us to live in the light of this. "Guard not only your words to each other, but also your attitudes towards each other."

Thought

I may not express my disapproval in words, but how often do I let out an exasperated sigh or a disgruntled grunt? Can I do something about that?

---

[159] Thomas à Kempis, *The Imitation of Christ* – Book 1, Chap 16, (Hendrickson, Massachusetts , 2004), p.16

Prayer

Let the words of my mouth and the meditation [musings] of my heart be acceptable in your sight, O LORD, my rock and my redeemer.[160]

DAY FIFTY-SIX

Patience and Steadfastness

5:10,11 (ESV)

As an example of suffering and patience, brothers, take the prophets who spoke in the name of the Lord. Behold, we consider those blessed who remained steadfast. You have heard of the steadfastness of Job, and you have seen the purpose of the Lord, how the Lord is compassionate and merciful.

Let's practice a little more patience as we stay a little longer with this. In verses 7 to 11, James uses the words "patient" and "patience" four times. James Adamson has described the word as meaning 'the self-restraint which does not easily retaliate'. Patience is not a gift; it is a virtue that is worked into us through the fires of suffering. A man who quickly retaliates defensively when under pressure shows very little evidence of the inner workings of God's grace in him.

James points us to some classic examples of patience. He mentions, first of all, the prophets who spoke in the name of the Lord. We are not sure who he has in mind, but we can recall a few names. We think of Moses, who suffered the prolonged leadership of a cantankerous and rebellious people. Then there was Jeremiah, the weeping prophet, who spoke for the Lord for twenty-three years without any response at all. We could then go to the list of unknowns in Heb.11:32-39.

The Greek word translated "suffering" here is unique to James. It is the word 'kakopatheia', and it means 'the suffering of evil or distress'. The experience of suffering actually resulted in the manifesting of patience. The two are, you see, inexorably linked. The patience that became an example to us was forged through years and years of disappointment, pain and rejection.

We don't like to talk of suffering, but St Therese of Lisieux wrote, "Suffering is the very best gift he has to give us. He gives it only to his closest friends." Closeness to Christ involves the sharing of his sufferings. This is a blessedness that the world knows nothing of. Again, James comes up with another word that is rare. It is the Greek word 'makarizō'. The only other time it is used is by the young Mary, who exclaimed, "Behold, from now on all generations shall called me blessed."[161] It means 'to be pronounced blessed'. This is not a secret or subjective sense of blessing; this is evidenced, pronounced and declared blessing. In other words, it is blatantly obvious. This blessing is reserved for those who remain steadfast under extreme pressure. It is for the ones who haven't folded, collapsed or denied their faith although all hell was set against them.

James does, in fact, name one man, and that is Job. Poor Job didn't know what had hit him. William Barclay makes an insightful comment here:

Few men have spoken such passionate words as he did; but the great fact about him is that in spite of all the agonizing questionings that tore at his heart, he never lost his faith in God ... His was no unquestioning submission; he struggled and questioned, and sometimes even defied, but the flame of his faith was never extinguished.[162]

At the end of Job's trial, the purpose of God shone through. There was a purpose to his suffering, and it became manifested. Also manifested was God's character. Another word unique to James is found here. It is 'polusplagchnos', and it means that God is 'abundantly, extremely compassionate'. His love is overflowing and passionate. Couple that with 'mercy', and you have a good idea of the One we deal with.

---

[161] Lk.1:48
[162] William Barclay, *The Letters of James and Peter*, The Daily Study Bible, (St Andrew Press, Edinburgh, 1993), pp.125

Thought

A.W. Tozer once wrote, "We want to be saved but we insist that Christ do all the dying."[163]

Prayer

Lord, if staying close to you means that suffering is part of the package, then please hold my hand tightly as we walk through it together.

---

[163] A. W. Tozer, *The Radical Cross: Living the Passion of Christ*, (Wingspread, 2006)

DAY FIFTY-SEVEN

Say What You Mean

5:12 (NLT)

*But most of all, my brothers and sisters, never take an oath,
by heaven or earth or anything else. Just say a simple yes or
no, so that you will not sin and be condemned.*

How many times have you and I heard this little phrase: "I swear to God"? It is used as a prefix to words like, "I am telling the truth," or, "If you ever do that again..." and many others. Again, James surprises us here by dropping in a sudden prohibition against yet another wrong way of using the tongue, and here he is almost quoting verbatim the words of his half-brother Jesus.[164] The correct use of the tongue is so important to James. What we say, and how we say it, reveals much of what is going on in our hearts.[165] In fact, throughout this letter, James is insisting on the respectful use of the tongue in all matters to do with relationships. We must respect each other, and above all, we must respect the name of God.

Why does James say, "...most of all..."? Why is this so important? We have to have a look at the practice of the Jewish people during that time. They would never, ever swear by the sacred name of God, but they would swear by everything else. Rabbi Akiba taught that "a man might swear with his lips, and annul it in his heart; and then the oath was not binding"[166]. His inward mental reservations could cancel the

---

[164] See Matt.5:33-37
[165] See Matt.12:34
[166] *Adam Clarke's Commentary on the Bible,* e-sword.net

words of his mouth. The question is, how on earth would you be able to build trust where that was going on?

Now there is nothing wrong in making an oath to ratify something. Even God swears by his own name.

> *By myself I have sworn; from my mouth has gone out in righteousness a word that shall not return: 'To me every knee shall bow, every tongue shall swear allegiance.'* [167]

Moses also taught:

> *It is the LORD your God you shall fear. Him you shall serve and by his name you shall swear.* [168]

The thing that God prohibited was the swearing by his name *falsely*.

> *You shall not swear by my name falsely, and so profane the name of your God: I am the LORD.* [169]

James was addressing a situation where people in the church were not speaking the truth when they made their oaths. Words easily tripped out of their mouths, whilst their hearts were somewhere else. This is what God hates. It's actually called lying. At the end of the verse James warns of the possibility of falling into condemnation. The word is actually 'hupokrisis', from which we get our word 'hypocrisy'. Promising one thing and meaning another is pure hypocrisy. Promising something, knowing full well that you don't mean to keep it, is pure hypocrisy.

James had an antidote to this sort of verbal and irreverent abuse of the name of God. He says, let your yes be yes and your no be no. Adamson writes:

> *...the point of this command ... is that the Christian does not need to swear, for his word is his bond: swearing is necessary only in a society where the truth is not reverenced.* [170]

---

[167] Isa.45:23

[168] Deut.6:13

[169] Lev.19:12

[170] James Adamson, *The Epistle of James*, The New International Commentary on the New Testament series, (Eerdmans, Michigan, 1976), p.195

We should, therefore, be people of our word, meaning what we say, and engendering trust among those with whom we have dealings. In that way, the name of God is seen to be respected and honoured.

Thought

The name of God and the name of Jesus are not meant to be used as expletives. They are to be loved and revered. Can our conversations and action drag these wonderful names into the mud?

Prayer

Dear Father in heaven, hallowed and sacred is your Name, now and always in my heart.

DAY FIFTY-EIGHT

Take Initiative in your Responses

5:13-14 (ESV)

Is anyone among you suffering? Let him pray. Is anyone cheerful? Let him sing praise. Is anyone among you sick? Let him call for the elders of the church, and let them pray over him, anointing him with oil in the name of the Lord.

We now come to a portion of James' letter that begs us to stop our reading for a while, and to get out our shovel and dig down. There are some incredible insights to be found here into the working out of the life of faith. This has been James' vision all along. Faith is to be outworked.

These verses link the reader with the whole theme of afflictions. A motif that runs right through the letter is that of trials, afflictions and suffering, and how we handle them. The Greek word used here for "suffering" is 'kakopatheō'. It is a very comprehensive word. One scholar translates it "calamities of every sort". It has been also translated "trouble" (NIV/Phillips).

The point is, it happens. We don't go looking for it, but it happens. The questions that we ask – did I bring it upon myself? did the devil afflict me with it? did God allow it to touch my life? – are somewhat out of place here. The bigger and better question is, what will we do when it does come? This passage of Scripture is all about taking initiative in our responses to the varying circumstances of life.

Life is full of ups and downs, whether we are Christians or not. There are moments and seasons of great peace and joy, and there are moments and seasons of disappointments and trials. Sometimes the road feels easy, and at other times the road seems very hard. In both these times, James encourages us to express ourselves to the Lord. It will do us good to note that in the first two scenarios he mentions – suffering and cheerfulness – we are exhorted to make reference to the Lord; and the hint is that we do it before anyone else gets to hear about it. In the third scenario, however – that of sickness – we are encouraged to turn also to the leadership of the church.

Suffering, then, should throw us into God. Unfortunately, though, the most natural response is one of grumbling, and this seems to be another theme of the letter. James says that if we are having a hard time, instead of moaning about it, we should pray about it. We should go straight to God about it – *first*. Do not think horizontally here, think vertically. Don't bottle it up, but express your feelings to the Father in prayer.

Cheerfulness, the other side of the coin, is a word that literally means 'good passions'. Phillips translates it "flourishing". James says here, "If that's how you feel, then sing!" Don't bottle it up, but express your feelings to the Father with a song. Isn't it sad, though, that a typical British response to someone singing is a cynical version of "What are you so happy about?" I love it when I hear someone quietly singing; it speaks of a heart at rest.

We need to learn to return to the Lord our thankfulness. It needs to be expressed. Here is a challenge to us all. We usually find it easy to sing with others, but to sing to the Lord personally can be a different thing. Such activity can change the atmosphere, and can bring about the lifting up of a dejected spirit.

The encouragement, then, is to take the initiative here in response to your circumstances.

Thought

Our reactions to the ups and downs of life tell more about us than our words and actions. The work that God does in us is always tested, and it is our responses to those tests that are measured in heaven.

Prayer

Dear Father in heaven, whatever life throws at me today, help me to respond quickly and easily in the Spirit, and not in the flesh.

DAY FIFTY-NINE

A Strategy for Sickness

A very balanced piece of Scripture is to be found in the book of Ecclesiastes. Solomon wrote, "For everything there is a season, and a time for every matter under heaven."[171] In the previous verse in James' letter, we looked at the two sides of a coin: suffering and cheerfulness. The first could turn us into a grumbler, and the second into being complacent. That's why James wants us to refer to the Lord, and express ourselves in the first instance, on both these issues. God is totally relevant to both.

On this third scenario that can touch the believer – the whole domain of sickness – we are encouraged to, not only turn to the Lord, but to also turn to the leadership. This does not suggest at all that we omit to talk to the Lord in the first instance, but that we are invited to include, in our seeking of help, the leadership of the local church. Technically speaking, it is worth noting that it is not that we *go to* the elders; we are to *call for* them, and the strong inference is that the elders will come to us. This speaks far more of pastoral visitation than prayer during a church service.

This needs qualifying. The word "sick" is the Greek word 'astheneō', and it means 'to be weak, feeble, to be without strength, to be powerless'. It can therefore mean anything that is disempowering or debilitating. In this sense, we could get the picture of one who is unable to make the journey to the gatherings. There are many who can make the journey, and should make the journey, and they can call upon the leadership within the gathering. Here, though, there is a strong sense of compassionate care. If they cannot come to the church, then the church will go to them. I think a strong pastoral response mechanism is being referred to here. The plural word "elders" also suggests that

---

171 Eccles.3:1

this is not the function of one solitary leader, but that it is to be done with others.

These elders were, firstly, to offer prayer. In the context of healing, this is the only place in the New Testament where prayer for the sick is called for. (We will, however, find prayer for the sick in the Old Testament.) All other references speak of *healing* the sick, not *praying* for them. Jesus never prayed for the sick; he healed them with a word, and he taught his disciples to do the same. The difference is enormous. Healing the sick is usually by a word of powerful and discerning command, whereas praying for the sick is usually by words of compassionate intercession. Of course, both are valid. By virtue of this verse, both methods are present in the Scriptures. But think about the first...

They were, secondly, to anoint with oil. The other reference to this in the New Testament is found in Mk.6:13, where Mark records of the disciples that "they cast out many demons and anointed with oil many who were sick and healed them". The oil seemed to act as a 'point of contact' – touch is important – it spoke of the anointing of the Spirit.

That this injunction is given to the elders of a local church is a proof positive that the ministry of healing was not locked into the apostolic era. Wherever and whenever there is godly leadership, there is the always the possibility of healing.

Thought

To those who worry about whether healing is for today, I heard the late John Wimber once say that those who pray for the sick see far more people healed than those who don't.

Prayer

Dear Lord, when I am sick, don't let me struggle alone. Help me to see that you have placed a wonderful resource in your church for me to tap into.

DAY SIXTY

The Prayer of Faith

5:15 (ESV)

And the prayer of faith will save the one who is sick, and the Lord will raise him up. And if he has committed sins, he will be forgiven.

There are numerous books that have written, and there are also various perspectives, on this whole area of healing, all of them claiming Scripture as the basis of their practice. They range from the belief that the ministry of healing actually finished when the last apostle died,[172] to the belief that every single prayer for the sick results in their healing. Somewhere in between these two extremes the truth is to be found.

This verse is connected to the previous verse by the little word "and". The context is that of a request that has been received for the elders to go and pray for someone who is sick. Upon their arrival, they are then to pray for the one who is sick, and anoint them with oil. James then goes on to speak of "the prayer of faith".

I think one of the best ways to understand this powerful little phrase is firstly to look at what it is not. It is obviously not the prayer of unbelief. That kind of prayer doesn't even get off the ground, let alone makes its way into the hearing of God. It is not even the prayer of hope. This kind of prayer trusts in the Lord, and knows that he is well able to answer the prayer, but is not sure how, when or if he will. The prayer of faith is one that is fully charged with faith.

I would link this kind of prayer with the manifestation of the Spirit found in 1.Cor.12:9. This faith of the Spirit is the *inrushing* of the same

---

[172] This view is called cessationism.

faith that Christ exercised in his ministry, and it is powerful in its effect. My personal belief is that such a prayer is ignited by a word from the Lord, and empowered by the Holy Spirit. The result is that the person is healed. I think that James sees faith needing to be expressed both in the sufferer – in that he calls for the elders – and in the elders themselves as they pray.

James uses the word "save". The Greek word 'sōzō' has a very wide spectrum of meaning including 'to save', 'to heal', 'to deliver' and 'to protect'. The context tells us, however, that James is referring to the physical healing of the afflicted person. He says that the prayer of faith will raise him up. The sense of the Greek gives the picture of one who is 'labouring and struggling under sickness'. The word "raise" is the Greek word 'egeirō', and it means 'to awaken, to arouse as from sleep'. The Lord will wake him and lift him up.

James then makes this interesting but important connection with sins. Note that it is not *since* the sufferer has committed sins, but *if.* Not all sickness is a direct result of sin, but, to be sure, some sickness is. If then there is sin behind the sickness, there needs to be confession and repentance before the prayer of faith can have effect. The promise is clear: not only will he be forgiven, he will also be healed.

Let us also be clear on this: unconfessed sin will resist the healing power of Christ. Deeply held resentments and unforgiveness toward others will resist the healing power of Christ. Acknowledging and confessing our sins, however, and also releasing others with forgiveness, will actually release the healing power of Christ into our own lives. Much healing has taken place under and alongside the experience of forgiveness. Forgiveness and healing walk hand in hand. It is my conviction that this ministry is still available to the church which lives and walks in faith. May it never become lost, but may the church of Jesus Christ ever be a prayerful and restorative resource to those who are in need.

Thought

Here's an interesting thought: Jesus promised that the things he did would be possible, not only to elders and leaders, but to all who believed in him.[173] That means both you and me!

---

[173] See Jn.14:12

Prayer

Pray with me: "Lord, I'm open to this…"

DAY SIXTY-ONE

The Power of Confession

5:16 (ESV)

Therefore, confess your sins to one another and pray for one another, that you may be healed. The prayer of a righteous person has great power as it is working.

Not only is there a sickness of body and mind, there is also a sickness of the soul. It is called sin. In the ancient mind, one was not far from the other. Most certainly, the fall of Adam and Eve ushered in much more evil than we could ever imagine. Sin has affected everything. Sickness and disease may not be the result of a specific sin, but their roots go right back into the Garden of Eden.

James is still in the context of healing and the confession of sins, and so we come across this next connecting word, "therefore". There is a difference, however, between the two verses. In verse 15, the conversation is between the sufferer and the leadership; here the conversation is with each other. What is James saying? I believe he is telling us that the community of the church of Jesus Christ should be the safest place on the earth for the burdened saint or sinner. Where else on earth can we, or should we, find a community of such deep love and sensitive understanding?

We are encouraged to confess our sins (literally, our falls and lapses and our 'side slips') to one another. We can, and should, firstly confess them to the Lord, but James is also encouraging the functioning of the body of the Lord. I quote at length Dietrich Bonhoeffer who wrote:

> *Our brother ... has been given to us to help us. He hears the confession of our sins in Christ's stead and he forgives us our sins in Christ's name. He keeps the secret of our*

confession as God keeps it. When I go to my brother to confess, I am going to God ... A man who confesses his sin in the presence of a brother knows that he is no longer alone with himself. He experiences the presence of God in the reality of the other person. As long as I am by myself in the confession of my sins, everything remains in the dark, but in the presence of the brother the sin has to be brought out into the light.[174]

The word translated "confess" is the Greek word 'exomologeō', and it carries the meaning of a full and frank confession, agreeing with God and another that it is sin that has been committed. It is, therefore, an issue that is 'brought out' into the open, into the light of God, and also into the light of another's face. One thing I have learned about the light of God is that it is, in the words of Psa.112:4, "gracious, merciful, and righteous". Notice the first two word: "gracious" and "merciful". As the people of God, we must ensure that we are so attuned to the ethos of heaven that people feel safe about confessing their sins among us.

There is also a huge responsibility here. What do we do with the sins that have been confessed to us? I believe that we take them together to the Lord and we ask for his healing of the issue in hand. We then forget them, just as God forgets them. They do not become 'stored information', maybe to be used later. The vulnerability of people must never be abused or exploited.

A word of wisdom is needed here. James is not saying that we confess to *anyone*, but rather *someone*. There needs to be careful choice about whom we open up our heart to. An open confession in the right ear has tremendous healing and releasing power.

Thought

One of the best gifts that you can give to another is your gracious, merciful, understanding and listening ears.

Prayer

Lord, I may not be my brother's keeper, but I can certainly be his helper and companion.

---

[174] Dietrich Bonhoeffer, *Life Together*, (SCM Press, London, 2015), p.87

DAY SIXTY-TWO

The Power of Prayer

5:17,18 (ESV)

Elijah was a man with a nature like ours, and he prayed fervently that it might not rain, and for three years and six months it did not rain on the earth. Then he prayed again, and heaven gave rain, and the earth bore its fruit.

This is one of the most loved and often quoted verses in the Bible, used to encourage prayerfulness. James is now expanding his theme. He has moved from healing to confession of sin, and now he writes of prayer. The whole passage, in fact, is about prayer, as if to say, whatever we do, or wherever or however we find ourselves, we need to pray. I get the impression that prayer, for James, is not something we occasionally refer to when in need, but is the very air that we breathe.

James is making a statement on the injunction to pray for one another. He is actually saying in effect, it works! There are, of course, different ways of reading this text. Let me quote a few.

The effective prayer of a righteous man can accomplish much.[175]
The prayers of the righteous have a powerful effect.[176]
Tremendous power is made available through a good man's earnest prayer.[177]

---

[175] NASB
[176] Moffatt
[177] J.B. Phillips

178

Prayer is a vast, and mostly untapped, resource to the church. We are in such a privileged position in that, as redeemed sons and daughters of God, we have free access to the throne of our Father in heaven. But it is not only a privilege; it is also a great responsibility. We are able to avail ourselves of heaven's resources, not only for ourselves, but for the benefit of others. Indeed, there are so many benefits to prayer – it brings us into intimate relationship with the Godhead, and it enables us to speak on behalf of others. And when we do, we are promised great results. Prayer, therefore, is firstly relational with the Lord, and then work on behalf of others.

The root of effective prayer is righteous living. There are times, I believe, when God puts his fingers in his ears when we pray, because we are knowingly out of relationship either with him or with others. In the issue of prayer, the walk definitely affects the talk. Also, the prayer of a righteous man does not consist of length, but depth. The ancient Jews used to say, "The prayers of the righteous are short." The biblical record gives credence to that.

James then gives an example of effective prayer, using the fourth of his Old Testament characters – Elijah. He does not seek to raise us up to Elijah's stature; instead he brings Elijah to us as a very ordinary human being. James is saying, "He was just like you, very human, often full of fears and an innate sense of inadequacy, and yet his prayers wrought powerful things in the earth." This rings true. God's power is usually released through the weakness of men.

"He prayed fervently." Literally, 'He prayed with prayer.' 'Proseuchomai proseuchē.' This is a Hebraism. The repetition of the noun gives intensity to the verb. This was no casual prayer; this was the pouring out of the soul. Desire was coming from the depths of his being. I am reminded here of Hannah, the mother of Samuel. Her words were not heard by Eli, but they were certainly heard by God. There was an intensity about them that moved heaven to listen and take action. She was pouring out her soul before the Lord. Any of us can do that, and when we do, we will have his ear.

Thought

Prayer is firstly a gift, by which we encounter and build our walk with the Lord, and then it is a responsibility on behalf of others.

Prayer

Lord, open my eyes, and capture my heart, and draw me into a life-shaping dialogue with you, and then, out of that conversation, show me the needs of those around me.

DAY SIXTY-THREE

The Restorative Community

5:19,20 (ESV)

My brothers, if anyone among you wanders from the truth and someone brings him back, let him know that whoever brings back a sinner from his wandering will save his soul from death and will cover a multitude of sins.

We are now coming to the end of the letter, and unlike most of Paul's letters, there is no doxology, nor are there any final greetings to named fellow co-workers. Instead, there is a passionate plea from the heart of a shepherd to his flock. It would help us to know that the biblical picture of a shepherd is more than a man out in front of the flock; it is also a man who is following the flock, taking note of the strugglers and the stragglers. See how David was called from "following" the flock in 2.Sam.7:8 and Psa.78:71. Here, we see the circular and varied movements of a true shepherd – leading with direction, ensuring and encouraging, nurturing and feeding.

Throughout the centuries, people have wandered from the faith. Scripture is replete with sad examples of this. It is not something new. People, having seen at first hand the miraculous power of God, have wandered away. Signs and wonders may provoke faith, but they do not sustain faith. Truth does that.

The word "wanders" is 'planaō', and the ESV has it perfectly. It also means 'to be misled' or 'to stray off the path'. It carries the idea of thoughtless slippage rather than open rebellion. I suggest that there is a three-stage slippage away from God.

Firstly, there is a slippage of the mind, where our grip on the truth is relaxed. We have to realise that truth is important. It is imperative that we believe the right things. Many have a weak grip because they

181

have very little knowledge of the truths of Scripture, and they are easily tossed to and from by "every wind of doctrine" as Paul would write in Eph.4:14.

Secondly, there is a slippage of life, where our walk is affected. Truth is designed to affect our way of life. Truth is to be practised. Truth accords with godliness, Paul told Timothy in 1.Tim.6:3; and where truth does not have sway, then our walk will be adversely affected. If we don't think right, then we will start to walk wrongly.

Finally, there is a slippage from our destiny in God. I do not believe that James is talking about the loss of salvation here, but he is talking about a loss of a God-given destiny. In a nutshell, we can arrive in heaven with a wasted life.

James says that if anyone is seen in spiritual slippage, then someone ought to bring him back. The word "someone" is deliberately indefinite, pointing to the fact that it is not just the responsibility of the leader, or the leaders, but it is the responsibility of whoever notices. There is a corporate community responsibility here.

To rescue a soul from death is to rescue and preserve someone's spiritual destiny. There are too many whose testimony is, "I could have been..." To have a multitude of sins covered, therefore, is to realise that however far we have fallen, we can return to an environment of compassion and full forgiveness. Love always covers a multitude of sins, and such is our God.

Thought

There is an old hymn, written by a twenty-two-year-old, that contains these words: "Prone to wander, Lord, I feel it..."[178] Out of a sense of personal fragility comes the best help for those who are struggling.

Prayer

In these days, O Lord, keep me from slippage in any way whatsoever.

---

[178] Robert Robinson, *Come, O Fount of Every Blessing,* Mission Praise, (Collins, London, 2009), No 1164

DAY SIXTY-FOUR

Concluding Remarks

I thought it fitting, owing to the rather abrupt ending of James' letter, to bring a few concluding remarks. Right at the beginning, we noted that James was the half-brother of Jesus. We asked ourselves the questions, "How could he have remained sceptical during all those years of growing up under the same roof as his elder brother?" "How could he have lived that close to Jesus and not have believed?" "What was it that blinded his heart?" The most probable answer is that Jesus did not meet James' Jewish expectations of the forthcoming Messiah. Predispositions, you see, can be so blinding. Yet at the resurrection not only James but all his other brothers were completely won over by the appearance of the risen Christ.

This letter majors on issues of faith. Faith is the heartbeat of the kingdom. The writer to the Hebrews tells us that "without faith it is impossible to please Him"[179].

James went on to write much about afflictions and trials, and stated that it is our faith that must interpret them. Our lives are wrapped up in the hands of God, and these things actually come to deepen and to sharpen our faith. Our response to them is vitally important. We are to "count it all joy" when they fall round us. Eugene Peterson interprets them as "gifts" that come to shape and mature our faith. This, indeed, is a biblical and faith-filled world view.

James also wrote much about the practising of our faith. Faith is authenticated by what we do, not by what we say or even proclaim. William Barclay wrote, "The one thing that James cannot stand is profession without practice, words without deeds."[180] James unpacks

---

[179] Heb.11:6

[180] William Barclay, *The Letters of James and Peter,* The Daily Study Bible, (The Saint Andrew Press, Edinburgh, 1976), p.75

this by firstly looking at our attitude towards the poor among us. Our attitude to those that the world writes off should reflect that of the Lord Jesus, who was known as "the friend of sinners". The apostle John picks this up when he says, "Little children, let us not love in word or talk but in deed and in truth."[181]

James wrote about our attitude towards the world. Faith does not take on board the values and the ways of the world. Faith sees through all this stuff to the invisible but tangible values and ways of God which have permanence about them.

James wrote much about the way we speak. Faith must fuel our conversations with each other. The tongue is to be touched and enflamed, not by hell, but with faith and love. Faith sees and speaks potential to that which seems hopeless; faith sees through difficult relationships to the deepening of team; faith constructs and encourages; through faith we sharpen each other.

James was probably a very straight-talking pastor with a great big heart. He was a man of prayer who would spend hours in the Temple, according to tradition, praying. He is one of those, I believe, of whom we are exhorted by the writer to the Hebrews to "consider the outcome of their way of life, and imitate their faith"[182].

Thought

The outcome of the life and the letter of James – that which he left behind him – has touched millions of lives. What will you and I leave behind us as a legacy? What will people remember us for?

Prayer

Lord, thank you for the life and thoughts of James. Please help me to take what I have read and turn it into a living reality in my own heart.

---

[181] 1.Jn.3:18
[182] Heb.13:7

Bibliography

Books and Commentaries

James Adamson, *The Epistle of James*, The New International Commentary on the New Testament series, (Eerdmans, Michigan, 1976)

William Barclay, *The Letters of James and Peter*, The Daily Study Bible, (St Andrew Press, Edinburgh, 1993)

Dietrich Bonhoeffer, *Life Together*, (SCM Press, London, 2015)

E.M. Bounds, *Power Through Prayer*, (Marshall Brothers Ltd, London)

Charles Bridges, *A Commentary on Proverbs*, (The Banner of Truth Trust, Edinburgh, 1977)

John Bunyan, *The Pilgrim's Progress*, (Oxford University Press, London, 1966)

R.W. Dale, *The Epistle of James and Other Discourses*, (Hodder & Stoughton, London 1898)

Gordon Fee and Douglas Stuart, *How to Read the Bible for All Its Worth*, (Scripture Union, Bletchley, 1993)

Johannes Jörgenson, *St Francis of Assisi*, translated by T. Connor Sloane (Image Books, New York, 1955)

Thomas à Kempis, *The Imitation of Christ*, Book 1, translated by Ronald Knox, (Burns and Oates, London, 1959)

Thomas à Kempis, *The Imitation of Christ*, Book 1, (Hendrickson Publishers, Massachusetts, 2004)

J. A. Motyer, *The Message of James: The Tests of Faith*, (IVP, London, 1970)

NIV Bible Commentary, Vol.2, (Hodder & Stoughton, London, 1994)

Eugene H. Peterson, *Working the Angles*, (Eerdmans, Michigan, 1995)

Eugene Peterson, *Subversive Spirituality*, (Eerdmans. Michigan, 1997)

A. W. Tozer, *The Radical Cross: Living the Passion of Christ*, (Wingspread, 2006)

Lucinda Vardey, *Mother Theresa – a Simple Path*, (Rider Books, London, 1995)

Kenneth S. Wuest, *Word Studies in the Greek New Testament, Vol.1*, (Eerdmans, Michigan, 1973)

Kenneth S. Wuest, *The New Testament – an Expanded Translation*, (Eerdmans, Michigan, 1961),

Electronic sources

Albert Barnes, *Notes on the Bible,* e-sword.net

Adam Clark, *Commentary on the Whole Bible,* e-sword.net

Matthew Henry, *Commentary on the Whole Bible,* e-sword.net

Jamieson, Fausset and Brown commentary, e-sword.net

The Preachers Commentary, e-sword.net

Robertson's Word Pictures, e-sword.net

Vincent's Word Studies, e-sword.net

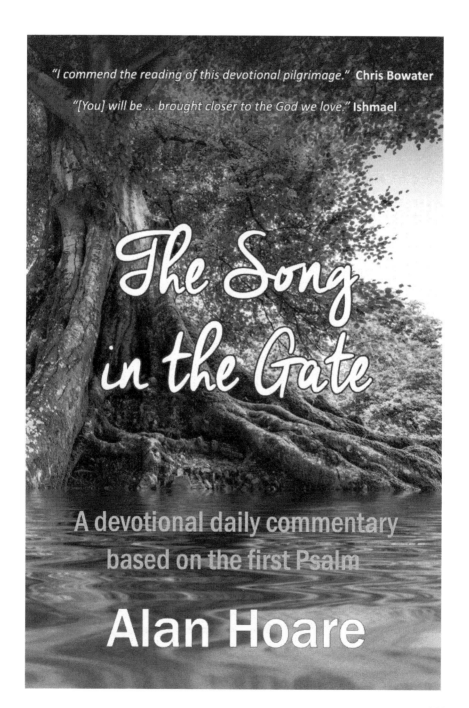

The Song in the Gate

"I commend the reading of this devotional pilgrimage." **Chris Bowater**

"[You] will be ... brought closer to the God we love." **Ishmael**

A devotional daily commentary based on the first Psalm

Alan Hoare